The Spiritual Power of Sound

THE SPIRITUAL POWER OF SOUND

THE AWAKENING OF CONSCIOUSNESS AND THE LAWS OF NATURE

Samael Aun Weor

GLORIAN

The Spiritual Power of Sound
A Glorian Book

© 2011 Glorian Publishing

Print ISBN: 978-1-934206-82-9
Ebook ISBN: 978-1-934206-67-6

Originally published in Spanish as "Mensaje de
Navidad 1965-1966" (named by students "La
Ciencia de la Musica").

Glorian Publishing is a non-profit organization.
All proceeds go to further the distribution
of these books. For more information, visit
gnosticteachings.org.

Contents

Illustrations

Chapter 1
Music

> "In the beginning was the Word, and the Word was with God, and the Word was God. The same was in the beginning with God. All things were made by him; and without him was not any thing made that was made. In him was life; and the life was the light of men. And the light shineth in darkness; and the darkness comprehended it not." - John 1: 1, 5

The sounding scale of the seven tones exists in the entire cosmos. The seven tones of the great scale, with the wonderful rhythms of the fire, resound in the entire universe.

Mahavan and chotavan are the fiery rhythms that maintain the universe firm in its march.

By singing in the temples at the dawn of creation, the seven cosmocreators celebrated the rituals of fire.

Without the magic of the Word, without music, without the creative Verb, the universe would not exist: "In the beginning was the Word."

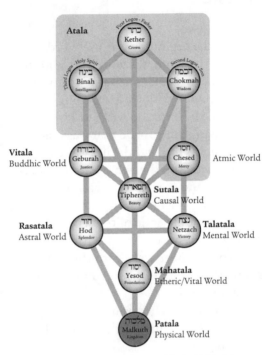

The Hindu Lokas in relation with the Kabbalah

Ancient [Asian] archaic traditions state that the knowledge regarding the sacred Heptaparaparshinokh (the Law of Seven) was revived many centuries after the Atlantean catastrophe by two initiate brother saints named Choon-Kil-Tez and Choon-Tro-Pel, who at the moment are in the Purgatory planet, almost ready to enter into the Absolute. In Eastern [Vedic] language it is stated that the Purgatory planet is the region of Atala, the first emanation of the Absolute [see diagram, left].

These two saints are twin brothers. The grandfather of these two initiates was King Konuzión, who wisely governed the ancient Asian country called Maralpleicie. The grandfather King Konuzion descended from a wise Atlantean initiate, a distinguished member of the Akhaldan Society. That society of wise people existed in the submerged Atlantis before the second transapalnian catastrophe.

These two wise holy brothers lived their first years of life in the archaic city of Gob, in that country named Maralpleicie. Afterwards, they moved to another country that later was called China.

These initiate brothers were forced to immigrate, leaving their native town when the sands began to bury it. Gob was buried by sands; thus, today that place is the desert of Gobi.

In the beginning, the brothers were only specialized in medicine; however, afterwards they became great sages living in what was later called China. These initiate brothers had the high honor of being the first investigators of opium. The brothers discovered that opium consists of seven subjective independent crystallizations with well defined properties. Later works came to demonstrate to them that each of these seven independent crystallizations consisted of another seven properties or independent subjective crystallizations, and each of these had another seven, and so on, indefinitely.

They were able to verify that there is an intimate affinity between music and color. For example, a colored ray directed upon any element of the opium transformed it into another of its active elements. The same outcome was obtained if instead of colored rays, the corresponding sonorous vibrations of the chords of a musical apparatus, known then with the name dzendvokh, were directed to any active element of the opium. It was scientifically verified that if we pass any colored ray through any active element of opium, the ray changes color—that is to say, the color matches the vibrations of the active element. If any colored ray is directed through the vibrations of the sound waves of the chords of the dzend-vokh, that ray changes to the color corresponding to the vibrations of the given chord. The dzendvokh was a formidable musical apparatus, with which it was possible to generally verify the power of musical notes on the opium, and generally upon all creation.

If a defined colored ray and sonorous vibrations—defined with complete exactitude—were directed upon any active element of the opium (chosen among those with smaller vibrations than the total vibrations of the colored ray and the mentioned sound) then the active element of the opium was transformed into another active element of the same opium.

It is intriguing to know that the seven subjective crystallizations of the opium corresponded to another seven, and to these another seven, and thus successively. It is also interesting to know that the septenary musical scale correlates to the septenary subjective crystallizations of the opium. Many experiments have also come to verify that the septenary subjective scales of human subconsciousness correlate to each septenary subjective classification of the opium.

If music can act on the septenary crystallizations of the opium, it is then logical to think that it can also act on the corresponding subjective septenary classifications of the human being.

Opium is marvelous because it receives all the powerful vibrations of the ineffable Protocosmos. Unfortunately, people have used opium in a very harmful and detrimental manner for human organisms. Many are those who used opium to fortify the tenebrous properties of the abominable Kundabuffer organ.

Many centuries after the sacred rascooarno (death) of the holy brothers, a very wise king existed who—based on the same theories of the mentioned initiates—constructed a musical instrument called lav-merz-nokh, with which he could verify many wonders related to music. The wonderful aspect of this musical apparatus is that it had forty-nine chords—seven times seven—corresponding to the seven times seven manifestations of the universal energy. This apparatus was formidable; it had seven musical octaves that were related to the seven times seven forms of cosmic energy. This is how the human race of that epoch knew, with flesh and bone, the "sacred Hanziano," that is, the Nirioonossian-World-sound.

All the cosmic substances that arise from seven independent sources are saturated by the totality of sonorous vibrations that the mentioned apparatus of music could cause to resound in space. We must never forget that our universe is constituted by seven dimensions, and that each of these dimensions has seven sub-planes or regions.

The musical apparatus constructed by King Too-Toz made all seven dimensions and all forty-nine energetic regions vibrate intensely.

In this day and age we already have formidable, revolutionary, and wonderful music based on the sound thirteen, yet we urgently need musical apparatuses like that of King Too-Toz.

We need to vivify the Nirioonossian sound vibrations of our world in order to intensify the cosmic sources of universal substances and to successfully initiate a new era.

The world was created with music, with the word, and we must maintain it and revitalize it with music, with the word.

The sacred law of the Heptaparaparshinokh serves as a foundation for the entire septenary musical scale.

It is urgent for all Gnostic brothers and sisters to comprehend this 1965 Christmas message—that is, the necessity to study music.

It is urgent for all the Gnostic brothers and sisters to always chant the five vowels I, E, O, U, A.

It is necessary to comprehend the value of the word and not to profane it with unworthy thoughts. It is just as bad to talk when one must be silent, as it is to be silent when one must talk. There are times when to speak is a crime; there are also times when to be silent is a crime. There are criminal silences, just as there are infamous words.

The Gods create with the power of the word, because, "In the beginning was the Word, and the Word was with God, and the Word was God."

There is a universal language of life spoken only by Angels, Archangels, Seraphim, etc. When the sacred fire blooms in our fertile lips made verb, the word becomes flesh in us. All the mantras known among the occultists are just syllables, letters, and isolated words of the language of the Light.

> "Whosoever knows, the word gives power to. No one has uttered it, no one will utter it, except the one who has the word incarnated."

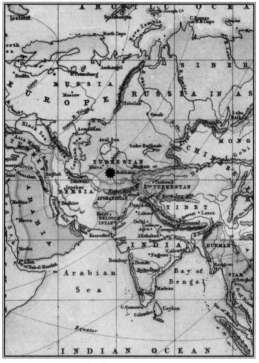

Map of Bokhara

Chapter 2

The Bokharian Dervish Hadji-Asvatz-Troov

The following is from a story related by G.

Once while traveling in that part of the Asian continent called "Bokhara," a sage coming from unknown places happened to meet and to establish a friendship with a certain "Whirling Dervish," whose name was Hadji-Zephir-Bogga-Eddin. This was a man who had the tendency to show enthusiasm for the theme of sacred esotericism. Hence, every time he met anyone along his way, he immediately talked about these types of studies. So, when he met the sage, his joy was great and he smiled happily. The theme they talked about was the ancient Chinese science named "Shat-Chai-Mernis."

In this day and age, nothing but fragments of a formidable totality is known about that mysterious science discovered by the great Chinese twin initiate brothers (whom we spoke of in chapter one of this message). In other times, when the Chinese twin brothers still lived in China, that mysterious science was called "totality of true information about the law of ninefoldness." Certain fragments of that august science remained intact and passed from generation to generation through many brethren initiated in the great mysteries. And so, the wise person of our story felt very happy when speaking with the dervish Hadji-Zephir-Bogga-Eddin about the ancient Chinese science Shat-Chai-Mernis, of which modern, Western, swollen-head types know nothing. This sage overflowed with enthusiasm when informed that he should go with Hadji-Zephir-Bogga-Eddin to talk about this with another dervish, a friend of his who resided in Upper Bokhara, far away from everyone, and who was occupied there with certain mysterious experiments concerning this very science. Thus, the Dervish Hadji-Zephir-Bogga-Eddin invited our wise person to have a stroll through the mountains of Upper Bokhara with the healthy and beautiful intention to visit the anchorite.

They walked for three days among steep mountains and solitary paths which led them to a small gorge high up in the mountains of Upper Bokhara.

According to the story, while in that mountain gorge, the Dervish Hadji-Zephir-Bogga-Eddin asked the sage to help him move aside a small stone slab. Once they had moved it, a small opening was revealed to the two men, from which two iron bars projected from its edges. The story states that the Dervish Hadji-Zephir-Bogga-Eddin put these bars together and began to listen; after a while, a strange sound was heard coming from them. Then, to the astonishment of the sage of our story, the Dervish Hadji-Zephir-Bogga-Eddin uttered some words into that opening in a language totally unknown to him.

When the Dervish had finished speaking, he and the sage moved the stone slab back to its former place and continued on with their stroll. They had to walk a distance among valleys and deep mountains until arriving at a certain place where they paused before an enormous stone. In a state of great tension, the Dervish Hadji-Zephir-Bogga-Eddin seemed to be waiting for something very special; then, suddenly, the enormous stone opened, forming a

mysterious entrance that led into a kind
of cave. Both men entered the cave and
began moving forward into its mysterious
depth, noticing that their way was illuminated alternately by gas and electricity.

After having walked a considerable distance within the cavern, they encountered
an elder of an indecipherable age with an
extraordinarily tall and thin body. He met
them with the customary greetings and
led them further into the interior of the
cave.

The Dervish's friend was a hermit
whose name was Hadji-Asvatz-Troov. The
old hermit led both men to a very comfortable section of the cave where they all
sat on felt that covered the floor. They
ate what in Asia is called cold Bokharan
"Shila-Plav" from clay vessels that the old
hermit brought them. The men conversed
with the old hermit during the supper
and naturally, the theme discussed was
the exciting Chinese science called Shat-
Chai-Mernis.

The science of this elder was the science
of vibrations. Everything that is, everything that has been, everything that will
be is within the science of vibrations. The
hermit had dedicated his life to the study

of vibrations, the Shat-Chai-Mernis. The hermit had very thoroughly studied the Assyrian theory of the great Malmanash, and the Arabian theory of the famous sage Selneh-eh-Avaz, and the Greek Pythagoras, and all the Chinese theories in general.

This man had constructed in a modified manner the monochord of Pythagoras, the famous apparatus of music with which Pythagoras made his experiments. That apparatus is very complex and is full of vibrometers that served him to measure the vibrations of the chords. The old hermit was a true sage who had constructed many apparatuses to measure the vibrations with exactitude.

"Indeed," said the elder, "in the very ancient civilization of Tikliamish, there once existed all kinds of special apparatuses to measure vibrations."

The hermit soon made several demonstrations with musical vibrations. With small bellows he blew air into the pipes of an apparatus of wind music, which then began a monotone melody of five tones. The vibrometers indicated with exactitude the number of vibrations. Next to the musical apparatus was placed a pot of flowers; when the hermit concluded the monotone music, the flowers in the pot were intact.

Thereafter, the old hermit moved from the old monochord to a grand piano, also provided with a vibrometer to measure the vibrations, and began to successively strike the corresponding keys of the grand piano, producing the same monotone melody. When the old hermit stopped striking the grand piano, the flowers that were full of vigor and beauty had withered. In this manner, the old hermit demonstrated the vibratory power of musical waves on matter.

The hermit divided the vibrations into two kinds: creative vibrations and momentum vibrations. The elder stated that special strings for the production of creative vibrations could be made from goat guts, and with the wind instruments like trumpets, flutes, etc., momentum vibrations can be obtained.

According to the story narrated to us, after giving some other explanations the hermit brought an envelope, paper, and a pencil for another experiment. On the paper he wrote something, placed it in the envelope, attached it to a hook hanging before his guests. He sat again at the grand piano and began just as before to strike definite keys, from which there was again produced a certain monotone melody. But this time, in the melody were evenly and constantly repeated two sounds of the lowest octave of the grand piano. After a little while, the Dervish Hadji-Bogga-Eddin could not sit still, for he began to fidget as he felt a frightful pain in his left leg. When at last the hermit finished playing the monotone melody, he turned towards the guest sage, and addressing him, said, "Friend of my friend, will you please get up, take the envelope off the hook and read what is written inside."

The sage stood up, took the envelope, opened it, and read as follows, "From the vibrations issuing from the grand piano, on each of you there will form on the left leg, an inch below the knee and half an inch to the left of the middle of the leg what is called a 'boil.'"

The elder requested both of them to expose the indicated places on their left legs. When they had done so, a real boil was displayed precisely on the place of the left leg of the Dervish Hadji-Bogga-Eddin.

However, much to the extreme amazement of the venerable Hadji-Asvatz-Troov, there was nothing whatsoever to be seen on the left leg of his other wise guest, as he had a different vibration. This was because he was a Master from another planet, and it is clear that the vibration of this genre was of another frequency, different from that which the elder carried in his body.

When Hadji-Asvatz-Troov ascertained that there was no boil on the left leg of his guest the sage, he immediately leapt from his place and cried out, "It cannot be!" and began to stare fixedly with the eyes of a madman at the sage's left leg. It was necessary then for this wise visitor from another planet to make him comprehend that nothing had failed, and that later, alone, he would tell him his secret.

It may seem incredible to many readers to know that inhabitants from other planets walk on our Earth. It is very likely that now they will sceptically laugh about it, nevertheless this is how it is. Our Earth has been visited throughout time by inhabitants of other planets. [Read *Cosmic Ships* by the author]. Ancient traditions state that the Master Sanat Kumara, founder of the great College of Initiates of the great White Lodge, came with his physical body from Venus. The sage of our story was a Master from another planet, yet he kept it secret.

In other times, there were wonderful musical instruments with which formidable experiments were performed. By knowing how to handle the vibratory waves of sound, it is possible to act upon every substance, upon all life. John 1:1 states:

> "In the beginning was the Word, and the Word was with God, and the Word was God."

Indeed, without sound, without the verb, without the Word, the solar system in which we live, move, and have our Being, could not exist.

In the dawn of life, the Cosmocreators worked in their temples with the sexual magic of the Word. The two fundamental forces cannot create by themselves; a third force is necessary in accordance with the sexual magic of the Word.

Any Master skillful in meditation can study cosmogenesis within the Akashic records, and thus verify for him or herself the liturgical work of the Cosmocreators at the dawn of life. The temples of the Cosmocreators and their work with the vibrations appear in the Akashic records visible to any illuminated one. Within each temple appear a priest and a priestess seated on their thrones in the internal East. In each temple there is a ground floor, on which are all the seats of honor and the columns of the temple. The Elohim mentioned by the sacred scriptures occupy that ground floor. This is the primeval Masonry. These are the workshops of the Cosmocreators. The priest and priestess chant along with all the Elohim of the temple, and their voices resound in the Chaos.

Thus, this is how the rituals of fire are performed at the dawn of life, and the three forces called masculine, feminine, and neutral scientifically vibrate, producing multiple phenomena within the primordial matter. Hence, the Great Mother, the prima matter of the Great Work, becomes fertilized, and the germs of all creation sprout forth. This is how the universe of Pleroma is born. This is how any solar system is born.

The sexual magic of the Word created this universe in which we live, move, and have our Being. In the beginning, our solar system was subtle. Later it became denser and denser until taking its present physical consistency. This universe is therefore a product of the vibrations of the Word, of music.

The Three Primary Forces on the Tree of Life (Kabbalah)

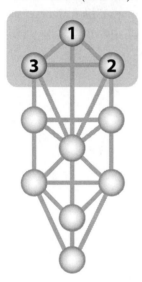

1
Aztec: Tepeu K'Ocumatz
Buddhist: Dharmakaya
Christian: The Father
Egyptian: Osiris-Ra
Gnostic: The First Logos
Hindu: Brahma
Kabbalah: Kether
Mayan: Huracan Kakulha
Nordic: Odin

2
Aztec: Ehekatl Quetzalcoatl
Buddhist: Sambhogakaya
Christian: The Son
Egyptian: Horus
Gnostic: The Second Logos
Hindu: Vishnu, Krishna
Kabbalah: Chokmah
Mayan: Chipí Kakulha
Nordic: Balder

3
Aztec: Tlaloc Quetzalcoatl
Buddhist: Nirmanakaya
Christian: The Holy Spirit
Egyptian: Osiris-Isis
Gnostic: The Third Logos
Hindu: Shiva
Kabbalah: Binah
Mayan: Raxa Kakulha
Nordic: Thor

Chapter 3

The Law of Three

Beloved, this Christmas of 1965 it is necessary for us to know in depth the Law of Three. It is urgent for us to know the place we occupy in the wonderful Ray of Creation.

The Son came into the world in order to save us. Thus, it is necessary to know what the Father is, what the Son is, and what the Holy Spirit is. All the sacred Trimurtis from all religions correspond to the three primary forces of the universe. The Father, the Son, and the Holy Spirit constitute a Trinity within the unity of life.

Isis, Osiris, Horus, and Brahma, Vishnu, Shiva, etc., are sacred Trimurtis that always represent the same three primary forces. All the cosmic phenomena, all creation, are based on the three primary forces.

Contemporary scientists recognize force and resistance, the positive force and the negative force, the positive and negative cells—that is to say, the masculine and feminine cells, etc.—but they ignore that any phenomenon, any creation, is impossible without a third, neutral force. It is entirely true, certain, that one or two forces cannot produce any phenomenon, yet scientists think that the positive-negative forces can produce all phenomena.

We can discover the three forces in action if we manage to study ourselves deeply.

Electricity is not only positive or negative; electricity also exists in its neutral form.

One or two forces can never produce any phenomenon. Thus, whenever we observe a halt in the development of anything, we can state with absolute certainty that the third force is missing there.

The three primary forces separate and unite anew; they are divided and cosmically multiplied.

Within the Unmanifested Absolute, the three primary forces constitute in an integral manner an indivisible and self-cognizant unity.

During cosmic manifestation, the three primary forces separate and unite; phenomena, worlds, universes, etc. are created in those points where the three unite.

In the Ray of Creation, these three forces seem like three wills, three consciousnesses, three units. Each of these three forces contains in themselves all the possibilities of the three; however, in their point of conjunction, each one of them only manifests one principle, whether the positive, negative, or neutral principle.

It is very intriguing to see the three forces in action: they separate, they move away, and soon they reencounter again in order to form new, different trinities that originate new worlds, new cosmic creations.

Within the Absolute, the three forces are the single Logos, the variety within a total unity. There, the Father, the Son, and the Holy Spirit constitute an omniscient and omni-merciful whole.

When speaking to his disciples about the Law of Three, Master G. stated:

> "Let us imagine the Absolute as a circle and in it a number of other circles, worlds of the second order. Let us take one of these circles. The Absolute is designated by the number 1, because the three forces constitute one whole in the Absolute, and the small circles we will designate by

the number 3, because in a world of
the second order the three forces are
already divided.

"The three divided forces in the
worlds of the second order, meet-
ing together in each of these worlds,
create new worlds of the third order.
Let us take one of these worlds. The
worlds of the third order, created
by the three forces which act semi-
mechanically, no longer depend upon
the single will of the Absolute but
upon three mechanical laws. These
worlds are created by the three forces.
And having been created they mani-
fest three new forces of their own.
Thus, the number of forces acting in
the worlds of the third order will be
six. In the diagram, the circle of the
third order is designated by the number 6 (3 plus 3).

"In these worlds are created worlds
of a new order, the fourth order. In
the worlds of the fourth order there
act three forces of the world of the
second order, six forces of the world
of the third order, and three of their
own, twelve forces altogether. Let us
take one of these worlds and desig-

nate it by the number 12 (3 plus 6 plus 3). Being subject to a greater number of laws these worlds stand still further away from the single will of the Absolute and are still more mechanical. The worlds created within these worlds will be governed by twenty-four forces (3 plus 6 plus 12 plus 3). The worlds created within these worlds will be governed by forty-eight forces, the number 48 being made up as follows: three forces of the world immediately following the Absolute, six of the next one, twelve of the next, twenty-four of the one after, and three of its own (3 plus 6 plus 12 plus 24 plus 3), forty-eight in all. Worlds created within worlds 48 will be governed by ninety-six forces (3 plus 6 plus 12 plus 24 plus 48 plus 3). The worlds of the next order, if there are any, will be governed by 192 forces, and so on." – In Search of the Miraculous

If we analyze in depth these mathematical calculations of the Master G., we must comprehend that the world of 96 laws is the first submerged plane of the abyss, and that the world of 192 laws

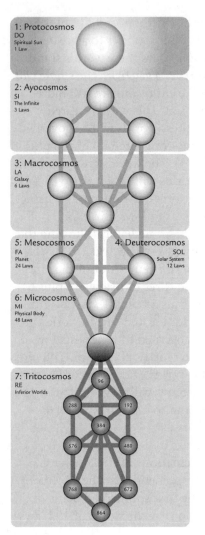

1: Protocosmos
DO
Spiritual Sun
1 Law

2: Ayocosmos
SI
The Infinite
3 Laws

3: Macrocosmos
LA
Galaxy
6 Laws

5: Mesocosmos
FA
Planet
24 Laws

4: Deuterocosmos
SOL
Solar System
12 Laws

6: Microcosmos
MI
Physical Body
48 Laws

7: Tritocosmos
RE
Inferior Worlds

96
288 192
384
576 480
768 672
864

The Seven
Cosmoses

corresponds to the second submerged plane of the abyss. The abyss is the mineral kingdom, and is located underneath the surface of the Earth. The abyss is the Greek Tartarus, the Hindustani Avitchi, the Roman Averno, the Christian Hell, etc. The abyss has other seven submerged atomic regions; these are the Atomic Infernos of Nature.

The Law of Three allows us to know how many laws govern each submerged region of Hell. If in the world of 48 laws, which is the cellular world where we live, everything is already mechanical and the will of the Absolute is not even remotely expressed, what then can we say about the mineral kingdom? The lost ones live in the mineral kingdom. Life in the mineral kingdom is very far from the will of the Absolute. The will of the Absolute is not even remembered within the submerged mineral kingdom.

The Ray of Creation begins in the Absolute and ends in the infernos. The proper order of the Ray of Creation is as follows:

1. Absolute
2. All Worlds
3. All Suns

4. The Sun
5. All Planets
6. The Earth
7. The Inferno

We regret to have to dissent with Master G. in regard to the subject matter about the Moon. Master G. thinks that the Ray of Creation begins in the Absolute and ends in the Moon. Master G. supposes that the Moon is a fragment split from the Earth in a remote archaic past. Master G. thinks that the Moon is a world in gestation and that it is fed from the terrestrial vitality.

We, who were active in the past Cosmic Day, know very well that the Moon was a world like the Earth, a world that was submitted to many evolving and devolving processes, a world that had life in abundance and that is already dead. The Moon is a corpse. The Moon belongs to the past Ray of Creation. The Moon does not belong to our present Ray of Creation.

The lunar influence is of a submerged subconscious type and controls the tenebrous regions of the terrestrial abyss. This is why in esotericism those regions are called submerged sublunar regions. Those are "the outer darkness where there shall be weeping and gnashing of teeth."

Moreover, we normally live in this cellular world of 48 laws (the Earth), yet it is very interesting to know that the germinal cell—from which by means of gestation the human organism develops—has 48 chromosomes.

If in this world—and in all the worlds of the third order created by the three forces, that already act semi-mechanically—the will of the Absolute is no longer done, much less is that will done in this world of 48 laws in which we live, move, and have our Being. Only a poor consolation remains for us (even though at heart it is terrifying): the fact that below us, under the Earth's surface, are worlds of 96, 192, and even many more forces, and which are tremendously more complicated and terribly materialistic, where the will of the Absolute is not even remotely remembered.

The Absolute creates its cosmic plan in the world of three laws, and thereafter everything continues mechanically. We are separated from the Absolute by 48 mechanical laws, which make our life frightfully mechanical and terribly boring.

If we build ourselves a true astral body (do not confuse this with the body of desires of which Max Heindel speaks), we liberate ourselves from half of the 48 laws, and are submitted to order of the twenty-four laws that wisely govern our planetary world. To build a Solar Body—that is to say, an authentic astral body—signifies in fact to be one step closer to the Absolute.

If after having built the astral body, we give ourselves the luxury of building the mental body (do not confuse this with the mental body that is normally used by the living and the dead, and which is of a lunar-animal type), we take another great step towards the Absolute; thus, we are submitted to twelve solar laws.

If we build the body of the conscious will or causal body (do not confuse this with the psychic essence which is placed within the lunar mind), then we liberate ourselves from the twelve solar laws, and we are submitted to the order of six cosmic laws; this signifies another step towards the Absolute.

The fourth step will lead us towards the Absolute, to the divine Protocosmos, which is governed by nothing other than the whole of the three laws. The

Protocosmos is Divine Spirit, and it is submerged within the bosom of the Absolute. All the suns and worlds of the Protocosmos are constituted with the divine substance of the Divine Spirit.

We can ascend or descend—return to the Absolute, or descend to the mineral kingdom. The souls that enter into the mineral kingdom are first submitted to the order of 96 laws, thereafter to 192, and as they are devolving in that submerged kingdom, accordingly, they become more and more complicated, with more and more laws.

Those who enter into the mineral abyss devolve, they go backwards, passing through the animal, vegetable, and mineral kingdoms. When the lost ones arrive at the mineral state, when they totally fossilize underneath the surface of the Earth, then in fact, they are disintegrated, they are reduced to dust. The abyss is the smelting crucible; it is necessary for the tenebrous ones to be disintegrated within the abyss so that their Essence, their Soul, becomes liberated and thus returned to their Divine Spirit, from whom they separated in a forgone day. In the smelting crucible, the petrified souls are smelted by the cosmic process which Henrik Ibsen symbolized as "The Button-Moulder" in *Peer Gynt*.

It is clear that the smelting of petrified and rigid forms which lost their developmental power is accompanied by frightful suffering and terrible, indescribable bitterness. The objective of the smelting crucible is to rectify the defective psychic product, to return it to its natural state of primeval purity, and to liberate it from the lunar bodies, after disintegrating the "I" by means of the submerged devolution. The ego and the lunar bod-

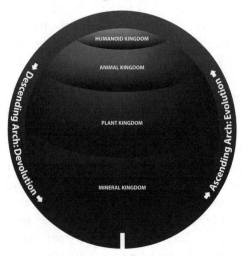

The Mechanical Kingdoms of Nature

ies are reduced to dust within the cosmic smelting crucible. Only by reducing the lunar ego and its bodies to dust, can the Essence, the Soul, the psychic principle, be liberated from the abyss.

A wise author said,

> "The descent into hell is, therefore, a backwards journey through devolution; a submersion within an always increasing density, through darkness, rigidity and within an inconceivable boredom of time; a backwards falling through the ages into the primitive chaos, from where the infinite ascent towards the knowledge of God must begin again from the beginning."

When addressing the abyss, *The Tibetan Book of the Dead* states,

> "If you cling to it, you will fall into the hells; you will be stuck in the mire of unbearable sufferings, without any escape."

Dante's *Inferno* is located within the interior of the Earth, and considers it formed by nine concentric spheres of increasing density. Those spheres are sublunar. Each one of those submerged spheres is governed by an overwhelming amount of laws that begin with 96, continue with 192, and multiply successively in accordance with the Law of Three.

A Master addressing hell said,

"This is the Hindu Naraka situated beneath the earth and beneath the waters. This is the Babylonian Aralu. The Earth of nonreturn, the region of darkness, the house within which the one who enters does not walk ahead, the way from which the traveller never returns, the house whose inhabitants never see the light, a region where dust is their bread and mud their food. This is the Greek Tartarus lead by the mouth of Earth where an amount of fire flows, together with enormous rivers of fire and many rivers of mud; an Earth cavern that is the greatest of all of them, and which crosses all the way through the earth. "Those considered incurable are thrown by the angel into the Tartarus where they no longer leave. It is the Egyptian Amenti represented in the cosmic plane of the great pyramid by a dark petreous chamber one hundred feet under the surface, whose floor was left distorted and of which a final passage leads to nowhere."

Inferno comes from the Latin word infernus, a word that means inferior region. The inferior region is not the cellular region in which we live. The inferior region is the interior of the earth, the submerged mineral kingdom under the surface of the terrestrial crust. Inferno is therefore the interior of the earth made up of seven regions; the lithosphere is the kingdom of minerals, the barysphere [centrosphere] is the kingdom of metals.

All human souls, a little sooner or a little later, identify themselves with the mineral kingdom by their persistence in crime, thus they end by entering into the mineral kingdom in order to suffer the fate of minerals.

The geological processes and geological time are frightfully slow and painful. Rare are the human souls that are resolved to liberate themselves from the 48, 24, 12, and 6 laws in order to enter into the Absolute. Humanity as a whole always prefers to pass from the 48 into the 96 laws. It is easier to enter into the world of 96 laws than to liberate oneself from the 48 laws. Regrettably, humanity always prefers what is "easiest." Yes, humanity enjoys making their hearts as hard as flint, hearts of stone, etc. Humanity enjoys to identify themselves with the mineral kingdom and to share the fate of minerals.

All religious infernos are symbols of the mineral kingdom. The atomic infernos of Nature are constituted by the mineral underworld. What is normal, what is natural for humanity—almost in its totality—is to enter into the mineral kingdom. The strange, the revolutionary, is that some souls Self-realize themselves, and after having liberated themselves from all the laws, enter into the Absolute.

To liberate one's soul from the 48, 24, 12, and 6 laws means to exert tremendous super-efforts, and people do not like to exert super-efforts. People always want what is most comfortable, what is easiest. Thus, this is why almost the totality of human souls—a little sooner or a little later—cease to be born in order to enter the underworld of 96 laws.

We can be liberated from the 48, 24, 12, and 6 laws only by means of the revolution of the consciousness. Regrettably, people do not like the revolution of the consciousness. People prefer to dance, drink, fornicate, adulterate, get drunk, get a lot of money, etc., since this is more comfortable for them than the revolution of the consciousness.

The revolution of the consciousness has three factors that people do not like:
· To die.
· To be born.
· Sacrifice for humanity.

To die is very difficult for people, because it is very rare to find someone who wants to die—that is to say, to disintegrate their beloved "I." Rare is the one who indeed is resolved to perform the sexual connection without the ejaculation of the Ens Seminis, with the purpose of building the legitimate astral body, the authentic mental and the true causal body or body of conscious will.

Rare is the one who is resolved to sacrifice himself for the salvation of the world.

People prefer to enjoy the pleasures of the Earth and to enter into the mineral underworld in order to suffer the fate of minerals, since that is easier, more comfortable, and simple. The revolution of the consciousness requires tremendous super-efforts, and people do not like anything that makes them uncomfortable.

Dimensions, Heavens, and Hells in Relation to Kabbalah

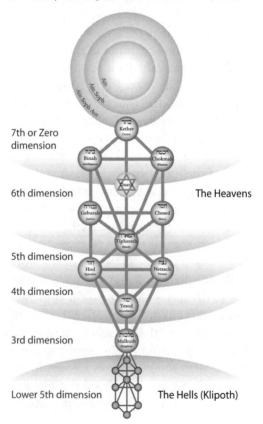

7th or Zero
dimension

6th dimension   The Heavens

5th dimension

4th dimension

3rd dimension

Lower 5th dimension   The Hells (Klipoth)

Chapter 4
Cosmic Materiality

With the proper scientific and mathematical combination of vibrations acting upon the prima matter of the Great Work, upon the chaotic and pre-cosmic Ens Seminis, the science of music originates seven orders of worlds with seven states of materiality.

Esoteric schools teach that there are seven planes of cosmic consciousness in the world. Likewise, we cannot forget that within the interior of our world, underneath the surface of the Earth, there are seven submerged atomic regions that relate to the atomic infernos of Nature, since the Holy Heptaparaparshinokh—the law of seven—is fundamental in everything created.

The sound vibrations of seven centers of gravity originated all the Trogoautoegocratic processes (the reciprocal nourishment of everything existent). In the end, these Trogoautoegocratic processes crystallized all the concentrations of worlds.

Music, the Word, originates what are called successive processes of the fusion of vibrations. Thanks to the law of the reciprocal nourishment of everything existent, and scientifically, under the impulse of sound vibrations, some vibrations flow from other vibrations. As well, cosmic substances of different densities and vivifications are united and disunited with each other, thus forming great and small, relatively independent concentrations. The outcome of all of this is the universe.

The first order of worlds is very spiritual and is within the bosom of that which has no name. The second order of worlds has a type of additional materiality. In the third order of worlds the materiality increases, and so on. In each one of the seven orders of worlds there is a sevenfold ranking of materiality.

The world—the universe in general—consists of vibrations and matter. $E = mc^2$: "Energy equals mass times the speed of light squared." "Mass is transformed into energy, energy is transformed into mass."

Matter is in a vibratory state. The vibratory speed is in an inverse proportion to the density of matter.

Each atom of the first order of worlds contains within itself only one atom of the Absolute; consequently, the first order of worlds is one hundred percent spiritual.

Each atom of the second order of worlds contains 3 atoms of the Absolute; as a consequence, the second order of worlds has a little more materiality, even though it still is very spiritual.

Each atom of the third order of worlds contains within itself 6 atoms of the Absolute; thus, clearly, the materiality is even greater.

Each atom of the fourth order of worlds contains within itself 12 primordial particles—that is to say, 12 atoms of the Absolute—and therefore it is logical to state that the fourth order of worlds has greater materiality than the three preceding orders.

Each atom of the fifth order of worlds has within itself 24 atoms of the Absolute, and so it is clear that its materiality is much greater.

We, the wretched intellectual animals, who are unfortunately condemned to the pain of living, really have the bad luck of existing in this remote and dark corner of the universe that belongs to a sixth order of worlds. Each atom of our world of 48 laws contains within itself 48 atoms of the Absolute. Thus, the materiality of our world is horrible, since everything that is obtained with supreme promptness in the worlds of 12, 6, or 3 laws is only obtained here—so to say—by sacrificial bleeding and with unspeakable sufferings.

Underneath us is the underworld where materiality is frightfully horrible. The first region of the abyss has atoms that contain within themselves—within each one—nothing less than 96 laws, 96 primary particles, 96 atoms of the Absolute. In the second region of the mineral kingdom, each atom has 192 atoms of the Absolute, and so on. Therefore, the mineral kingdom is frightfully materialistic. Thus, this is why life under the Earth is indeed an inferno. Nevertheless, it is good to clarify that the inferno has its mission, since it is the cosmic crematorium, and therefore it is necessary.

Somebody stated, "Inferno comes from the Latin word infernus, meaning 'inferior region', and therefore the inferno is this world in which we live." That person was mistaken, because this cellular region in which we live is not the inferior region; we live in the sixth order of worlds governed by 48 laws, and in accordance with the law of seven the seventh is the bottom. We already know that the seventh order of worlds is the underworld, whose first region is governed by 96 laws.

The inferno is not a place with flames. The inferno is the underworld. However, it is logical to state that the flames of passions burn within the underworld. All the religious infernos are only symbols of the underworld.

Time in the mineral kingdom is a time of rocks, a frightfully slow and terribly boring time. Each small event in the underworld is equivalent to 80 years, 800 years, 8,000, and 80,000 years.

The lost ones of the ancient Earth-Moon are named Lucifers, Ahrimans, and Anagarics with red turbans. They still live within that submerged mineral kingdom, and believe that they are doing very well, that they are progressing. The lost ones always believe that they are doing very well, and they are filled with very good intentions.

Christ Divides the Sheep from the Goats

*And before him shall be gathered all nations: and he
shall separate them one from another, as a shepherd
divideth [his] sheep from the goats: And he shall set
the sheep on his right hand, but the goats on the left.
Then shall the King say unto them on his right hand,
"Come, ye blessed of my Father, inherit the kingdom
prepared for you from the foundation of the world..."
[...] Then shall he say also unto them on the left hand,
"Depart from me, ye cursed, into everlasting fire, prepared for the devil and his angels..." - Matthew 25*

Chapter 5
Nature

The wretched intellectual animal falsely called "human being" can develop all of his hidden possibilities—if this is what he wants—nonetheless, the development of all those possibilities is not really a law. The law for the human machine is to be born, to grow, to reproduce, and to die within the vicious circle of the mechanical laws of Nature.

Jesus Christ, whose nativity we celebrate December 25th with rituals and festivity, said the following in Luke 13:24:

> "Strive to enter in at the strait gate: for many, I say unto you, will seek to enter in, and shall not be able."

Strait is the gate, and narrow is the way, which leadeth unto the development of all the possibilities of the human being, and few are those who find that gate and that way.

In fact, the path that leads to the development of all the hidden possibilities of the human being goes against Nature, against the Cosmos, against the common and ordinary social life, against oneself, against everything and against everyone. This explains why this path is so difficult and exclusive. For good reason it has been called "the path of the razor's edge." This path is very bitter, more bitter than bile. It is the opposite of ordinary life, everyday life. It is based on another type of principle. It is submitted to other laws.

The wretched intellectual animal falsely called "human being" can develop all of his hidden possibilities—if this is what he wants—nonetheless, his possibilities can remain without any development whatsoever and can even be totally lost. Many pseudo-occultists and pseudo-esotericists wrongly suppose that those possibilities can be developed by means of the wise law of evolution, yet that concept is totally false, because no mechanicity can develop all of our latent possibilities. The realization of the Inner Self of the human being is never the outcome of any mechanicity, but the end result of a cognizant work made with extreme patience and pain, by our self and within our self. We can develop all our hidden possibilities only by means of successive and interrupted self-cognizant works within our self.

The law of evolution and progress, and the law of devolution and retrogress, are two mechanical laws that work in a harmonious and coordinated manner in all of Nature. Everything evolves and devolves, advances and retrogrades. There is evolution in all the organisms that are born and develop. There is devolution in all the organisms that age and die.

In the everyday, routine life of all of those pseudo-esoteric, occultist, spiritualist, scientific, etc., schools, there is nothing that has all the possibilities of the path. Hence, sooner or later they can only lead us to death; they cannot take us to any other place. The path of the razor's edge is filled with dangers within and without. The one who finds the path is very rare; yet, it is even rarer to find someone that does not leave the path and arrives at the goal.

In the world there are many pseudo-esoteric and pseudo-occultist schools with very good intentions, and precious studies that do not harm anyone and benefit many, but they do not know the path. Indeed, the path is very hidden, narrow, and—what is even worse—frightfully difficult. Nobody likes the path, but only the few; the pseudo-esotericists, pseudo-occultists, and devotees of many very beautiful sects abhor the path and qualify it as black magic.

The mechanical evolution of the intellectual animal mistakenly call "human" is necessary for Nature until certain very well-defined point. Beyond this point, the mechanical evolution of the human biped becomes not only unnecessary but also detrimental for Nature.

The evolving and devolving processes of humanity correspond with the periods of evolution and devolution of planets in space. Essentially, we will state that in fact humanity does not evolve; many changes take place in the periphery of human consciousness, but not in the center of human consciousness.

The multitudes that acclaimed Nero and requested the crucifixion of Jesus Christ, the multitudes that enjoyed stoning the prophets, are still the same. They have only changed their bodies and customs. Their essence remains the same; it has not progressed.

Sometimes planets produce evolving changes, sometimes devolving changes in the periphery of the intellectual animal.

New civilizations rise and fall; yet the
Soul, the Essence, remains the same.

This miserable human anthill lives on
the Earth's surface in order to fulfill the
purposes and necessities of Nature. The
Earth does not waste anything, because
it wants to live and to use equally the
products of evolution as the products of
degeneration, even when in each case the
intentions are totally different.

Indeed, the intellectual animal can
become human by means of the realization of the intimate Self. Nevertheless, the
Self-realization of all the human masses is
not only something impossible, but moreover something harmful for the planet
upon which we live. Nature does not need
the realization of the intimate Self of the
human being, since this is even in opposi-
tion to its own interests. Thus, this is why
certain very special forces exist—unfortunately black—that violently oppose the
realization of the intimate Self of the
human multitudes.

In the epoch of the famous Tikliamish
civilization that existed many centuries
before the birth of Babylon, the life of this
humanity in general was divided in two
currents. The Christian Gospels speak

about two flocks—namely, the flock of the sheep and the flock of the goats. There is no doubt that the totality of human beings who populate the Earth belong in fact and by their own right to the kingdom of the goats.

Nature swallows its own children. Nature eats its goats, which are as numerous as the sands of the sea. Human life on the Earth flows in two currents: the current of sheep and the current of goats.

Indeed, the person who truly possesses the Being—the Innermost—follows the current of the river of life. Yet the person who does not possess the Being follows the current of the tenebrous river of death. The river of life is lost in the ocean of the Universal Spirit of Life. The river of death is lost between the gaps of the deepest regions of the Earth. The Earth needs nourishment and the river of death delivers it through its black waters.

The devolving processes that take place inside the planet Earth could not exist without the activity of the goat-skinned men and women who enter into the subterranean world. Behind all the vital mechanism of the world, behind all those chemical processes that structure the hard rock is the collective psyche of the goat-skinned men and women. Those tenebrous ones give physical consistency to iron, flint, and granite. If by any procedure we extracted from the infernos (the mineral kingdom) all the tenebrous ones who inhabit it, then the hard rock would lose its consistency, its hardness, and would become elastic, plastic, and useless; then its end would be an inevitable fact.

The first liberation of man consists precisely in the possibility of passing from the tenebrous current that is predestined to disappear within the profundities of the Earth, to the luminous current that must end within the ocean of the Great Light.

To pass from the black current into the white current is not easy. For that to happen it is urgent to resign from everything that is pleasant to us and which seems a blessing, to resign from all of that which seems to us very romantic and precious, etc. It is necessary to die to the world, to dissolve the "I," to abandon all of that which has a delightful and passionate flavor, etc.

It is necessary to be born, and this is a work with the grain, with the seed: a sexual problem. It is indispensable to love our fellowmen and to totally sacrifice our self for them. The path is more bitter than bile, and it is not convenient for Nature because it is contrary to its designs.

Humanity nourishes the mineral kingdom (inferno). Humanity is part of the organic life of the Earth; it is the nourishment of the Earth. Thus, if all of humanity were to become Self-realized, this would be fatal for the mineral kingdom. This is why Nature is opposed to the realization of the inner Self of the human being, because this is contrary to its own interests. What is normal, what is natural, is for the mineral kingdom to swallow humanity.

Jesus Christ said, "Of a thousand that seek me, one finds me; of a thousand that find me, one follows me; of the thousand that follow me, one is mine."

Chapter 6

The Revolution of
the Consciousness

The revolution of the consciousness is
the Fifth Gospel.

We urgently need a radical, total, and
definitive change. This is only possible by
means of the revolution of the consciousness.

The realization of the Inner Self is only
possible in isolated individuals, with the
help of knowledge and suitable methods.
Such an inner revolution can only happen
within the individual, and is in fact contrary to the interests of Nature.

The development of all the possibilities
hidden in the intellectual animal is not
necessary. It is only and exclusively for his
own welfare. Neither Nature, nor anyone
is interested in the development of such
individual possibilities.

What is the most grave of all of this
is that now nobody is obligated to assist
the revolutionary individual. Nobody has
the slightest intention to help this class
of revolutionary. One is completely alone,

and if a revolutionary Master resolves to guide us, this is really to have had much luck.

The tenebrous forces that are resolutely against the realization of the Inner Self among the great human masses are also resolutely and even violently opposed to the revolutionary individual's realization of the Inner Self. Therefore, every revolutionary individual must be sufficiently astute in order to deceive the tenebrous forces, since the human masses unfortunately cannot do it. Only the revolutionary individual can manage, by his wits, to be readier than these tenebrous forces.

Obligatory or mechanical Self-realization does not exist. The realization of the Inner Self of the human being is the outcome of a conscious fight. Nature does not need the realization of the Inner Self of the human being, it does not want it, it detests it. Thus, Nature fights against it with its best weapons.

The realization of the Inner Self can only be an urgent necessity for the revolutionary individual, when he realizes his horrible situation and the abominable fate that awaits him, which is the fate of being voraciously swallowed by the mineral kingdom.

The revolution of the consciousness is only possible in the sense of winning, conquering, our own latent possibilities, our own hidden treasures. If all of the human species wanted to obtain what is theirs by right, then the realization of the Inner Self would be impossible, because what is possible for the revolutionary individual is impossible for the masses.

The advantage that the separated revolutionary has is that, indeed, he is too small. The existence of one more-or-one-less-machine does not have the smallest importance to the aims of great Nature. If one microscopic cell of our body revolts against us, that does not have the smallest importance, but if all the cells of our body revolt against us, then yes, the matter becomes serious and we go to the doctor in order to fight against this revolution with all the weaponry of science. Exactly the same thing happens in an isolated individual: such a one is too small to influence all the life of the planetary organism upon which we live, move, and have our Being. Therefore, those who affirm that by means of the evolution of Nature all human beings will sooner or later arrive at the realization of the Inner Self are tremendous liars, fraudulent deceivers, because mechanical Self-realization has never existed, and will never exist.

The realization of the Inner Self is the revolution of the consciousness, and the consciousness can never unconsciously revolt. The revolution of the human being is the revolution of one's own will, and this could never be a mechanical type of involuntary revolution. The realization of the Inner Self is the outcome of supreme, voluntary, and perfectly self-cognizant efforts. The realization of the Inner Self demands tremendous individual super-efforts, and these are only possible by means of the revolution of the consciousness.

Jesus Christ, whose nativity we celebrate this night, December 24th, 1965, never promised the kingdom to all human beings. Jesus emphasized the difficulty of entering the kingdom.

> "Every tree that bringeth not forth good fruit is hewn down, and cast into the fire." - Matthew 7:19

"For many are called, but few are chosen." - Matthew 22:14

"Again, the kingdom of heaven is like unto a net, that was cast into the sea, and gathered of every kind: Which, when it was full, they drew to shore, and sat down, and gathered the good into vessels, but cast the bad away. So shall it be at the end of the world: the angels shall come forth, and sever the wicked from among the just, And shall cast them into the furnace of fire [the mineral kingdom]: there shall be wailing and gnashing of teeth." - Matthew 13:47-50

Thus, only the truly revolutionary human being can enter the kingdom of white magic, the kingdom of esotericism, the magis regnum, regnum Dei. Jesus said it:

"The kingdom of heaven suffereth violence, and the violent take it by force." – Matthew 11:12

What is normal, what is natural, is that the race of intellectual animals, falsely called human, falls into the abyss in order to be devoured by Ammut, the devourer of the dead, whose crocodile jaws prefigured all the mouths of Hell of the Middle

Ages. This abominable monster, a symbol of the mineral kingdom with its seven atomic, submerged regions, who is partly reptile, partly lion, and partly hippopotamus, and emerges—according to the sayings of the Egyptians—from an ardent, fiery lake, is the devourer of hearts, the devourer of the unvindicated ones, and who—for the Egyptians—symbolized a kind of terrible cosmic vulture, whose function was to consume the remainders or despoliation of humanity.

Therefore, it is not rare for someone to enter the mineral kingdom; that is normal, given that the mineral kingdom needs that someone for its psychic nourishment. What is rare indeed is for someone to enter the kingdom of high magic, because only the revolutionaries of the consciousness enter into this kingdom, ardently, like the fire.

Chapter 7

The Three Factors

The three factors of the revolution of the consciousness are:

· To be born.
· To die.
· To sacrifice for humanity.

By all means, if Christ is not born within us, it is impossible to celebrate the Nativity of the heart. Whosoever wants to jubilantly celebrate the Nativity of the heart must build the superior, existential bodies of the Being. We can incarnate the intimate Christ only by creating the superior, existential bodies of the Being.

We already stated in all of our former messages that the present internal bodies—mentioned by the pseudo-esoteric and pseudo-occultist schools—are useless for the realization of our Inner Self, because they are lunar bodies.

We urgently need to build the solar bodies—the superior, existential bodies of the Being—and the creation of these solar bodies is only possible by practicing the Maithuna (Sexual Magic), with the objective of transmuting the famous Sexual Hydrogen Ti-12. We can only build the superior, existential bodies of the Being with Sexual Hydrogen Ti-12.

It is totally impossible to incarnate the Being if we do not possess the solar bodies, if we did not build them by means of Maithuna (Sexual Magic). We have already given the clue of Maithuna many times; however, for those who do not know it we must repeat it in this 1965-1966 Message: the sexual connection of the lingam-yoni, without ever spilling the Ens Seminis during our entire life.

In past messages, we have greatly clarified this; we have also said plenty about the necessity of knowing how to die. Mystical death—the death of the "I," of the myself, of the self-willed—is urgent. We have explained to satiation that the "I" is a legion of devils. It is urgent to disintegrate that "I," to reduce it to dust, with the single purpose that within us will only be the Being. It is clear that in order to disintegrate the "I" a revolutionary ethics based on psychology is necessary. We have taught such ethics, we have taught such psychology. The dissolution of the "I" is a radical, total, and definitive revolution.

The third basic factor of the revolution of the consciousness consists of sacrificing oneself for humanity, of showing the way to others. This is charity very well understood; this is love.

We have greatly explained and we have said much in our former messages about the three basic factors of the revolution of the consciousness, yet people are lukewarm, so Christ said:

> "So then because thou art lukewarm, and neither cold nor hot, I will spew thee out of my mouth." - Revelation 3:16

Each pseudo-occultist and pseudo-esotericist reacts to the three factors of our Fifth Gospel according to their age, mental conditioning, prejudices, passions, weaknesses, etc.

The people full of sexual power prefer to begin the work with the Maithuna, but put in oblivion the death of the "I" and the sacrifice for humanity.

The wretched, decrepit old men and women, as well as the impotent and sick, prefer to begin the work with the dissolution of the "I," but they commit the mistake of confusing our revolutionary ethics with that false, lukewarm, subjective, insipid, incoherent, and absurd morality, so postured by all the little brothers of the different pseudo-esotericist and pseudo-occultist schools.

Finally, there are some little brothers and sisters from those cited schools who prefer to begin their work by sacrificing themselves for humanity, by doing something for their fellowmen; yet, they commit the mistake of forgetting the dissolution of the "I" and the Maithuna.

There are also very many cases of sexually potent people, full of life, who prefer to begin their work with the dissolution of "I," but who are not revolutionary. They want to dissolve their "I" with the false morality of pinheads, with that previously mentioned old-fashioned morality that is abundant amongst the little brothers of all of those pseudo-esoteric and pseudo-occult schools. In general, these people usually state with a certain self-righteousness: "What we need first is to be moral, because without morality there is nothing. Everything else can come later." Thus, this is how they escape, they flee, in order to take refuge in that heavy and horrible inertia of false morality.

It is clear that all of those people inevitably fail. Even if they had millions of lives in this world, at the end they would stop having physical births in order to enter into the mineral kingdom. The abyss is full of sincere but mistaken people, filled with very good intentions.

It is correct for old and impotent people to postpone the Maithuna for their future life and to begin their work with the dissolution of their "I"; yet, it is not correct to want to dissolve their "I" based on sanctimoniousness.

It is correct that people full of sexual potency begin right now to work with the Maithuna in order to build their solar bodies, but is not correct for these people to not worry about the dissolution of their "I," nor about sacrificing for humanity.

It is correct that we sacrifice ourselves for humanity, but it is not correct to forget about the dissolution of the "I" and the creation of the superior, existential bodies of the Being. The inner realization of the Self is only possible by working with the three basic factors of the revolution of the consciousness.

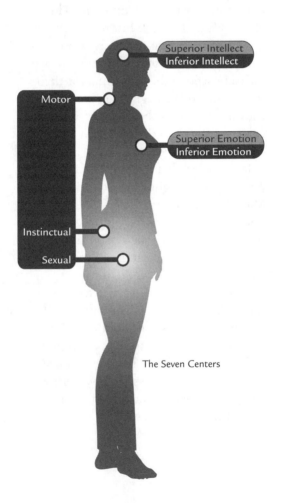

Superior Intellect
Inferior Intellect

Motor

Superior Emotion
Inferior Emotion

Instinctual

Sexual

The Seven Centers

Chapter 8
Abuse of Sex

On this Christmas 1965-1966, it is urgent for us to comprehend in an integral manner the necessity of liberating ourselves from this world of 48 laws in which we live, if what we want is to not degenerate and fall into the horrifying world of 96 laws. Indeed, the study of the 48 laws in which we live is a very profound study. If we want to liberate ourselves from the 48 laws, then we must study these laws within ourselves.

In the beginning, we comprehend that we are controlled by innumerable laws that were created by ourselves and by the people who surround us. Later we will comprehend that we are enslaved by these laws. Thus, when we began to liberate ourselves from all of those boring laws created by society, it is clear that our fellowmen become our enemies, because of the fact that we no longer coincide with them in regard to their mistaken manner of thinking, feeling, and acting.

The revolution of the consciousness is terrifying; this is why it is instinctually, mortally hated by our fellowmen, since they do not know it. To make the sexual energy return inwardly and upwardly, to dissolve the "I" and to give our life for the sake of others, is something strange and exotic for the goat kids who are as numerous as the sands of the sea, and who live amongst us. Yes, the revolution of the consciousness is impossible for the abusers of sex. Surely, goat-skinned people are not willing to leave their sexual abuses.

The human machine has seven centers—five inferior and two superior—which seems likely to be unsuspected by people. Let us study the five inferior centers: the intellectual center is the first, the emotional center is the second, the center of movement is the third, the instinctual center is the fourth, and the sexual center is the fifth.

Undoubtedly, it is certain that sex is the center of gravity of all human activities. Moved by sex, people go to church; moved by sex, they meet at the café; moved by sex, they dance. When a man finds his woman companion and they sexually unite, then society has begun.

The mechanicity of sex is frightening; regrettably, the intellectual animal does not want to comprehend it. When we acquire cognizance of sex and its functions, when we practice Maithuna (Sexual Magic), then that mechanicity disappears and we begin to tread the path of sexual regeneration.

Sex has the great power to enslave and the great power to liberate totally.

The new birth—about which Jesus spoke unto Nicodemus—depends totally upon sex. The internal Angel must be born from sex, and we can achieve this only by means of Maithuna—yes, if we yearn for a true Nativity, then we need the God Child of Bethlehem to be born within us, and this is only possible with Maithuna.

Sex works with and produces the marvelous Hydrogen Ti-12: it is seed, the seed within which the internal Angel abides in a latent state. We already explained that with the transmutation of Hydrogen Ti-12 we can build the true astral body, the true mental body, and the legitimate causal body. In our former messages we have spoken very clearly about this. No abuser of sex will be able to build the existential bodies of the Being. Hence, this is why after physical death those wretched individuals continue to exist with lunar vehicles. Listen: only when we build the solar bodies—the existential, superior bodies of the Being—can we then liberate ourselves from the 48 laws.

There is abuse of sex when sexual energy acts through the other centers of the human machine, or when the energy of the other centers acts through the sexual center. Each center of the human machine should work with its own energy; but regrettably, the other centers of the human machine steal the sexual energy. There is abuse of sex when the intellectual, emotional, motion, or instinctual centers steal sexual energy. What is most serious of all of this is that in like manner, in order to be able to work, the sexual center steals energy from the other centers. All of this is abuse of sex.

When the sexual center works with its own Hydrogen Ti-12, then it can be transmuted in order to build the existential bodies of the Being. Regrettably, people abuse sexual energy. People take pleasure in disorder and in the squandering of Hydrogen Ti-12.

To discover people's abuse of sex is easy, since when there is abuse of sex, the intellect, emotion, movement, and instinct have a certain special "flavor," a certain unmistakable nuance, a certain passion, a certain vehemence that leaves no room for doubt. This can be seen in all of the mental tactics of those gentlemen of war, in bullfights, in the passionate efforts of soccer players during the Olympic Games, in the violent, passionate instincts of people. Everywhere there is a squandering of diabolic intellect, violent emotions, passionate movements, passionate races of cars, horses, bicycles, Olympic games, etc., and likewise of beastly instinctual actions. It is clear that in all of this is the abuse of sex.

The most critical of all of this abuse is that the sexual center is forced to work with heavier Hydrogens that correspond to the other centers. When the sexual center is forced to work with Hydrogens, like 24, 48, etc., then it is impossible to build the superior existential bodies of the Being.

Those who enjoy watching pornographic films, novels, and paintings utilize the sexual energy through the thinking center, and it is clear that they hang about with the tendency of satisfying themselves solely with that sexual fantasy, and sooner or later acquire the psycho-sexual type of impotence, which is the impotence of those who lamentably fail when they really are going to perform the sexual act.

When the emotional center steals the sexual energy, then emerges stupid sentimentalities, jealousy, cruelty, etc.

When the center of movement works with the Hydrogen Ti-12, stolen from sex, then the abusers of the center of movement appear, like football players, circus acrobats, cyclists of great races, etc.

When the instinctual center steals the sexual energy, then there is instinctual, passionate squandering through violent acts.

Indeed, abuse of sex ends when we establish a "permanent center of gravity" within ourselves.

We have already stated—and now we repeat again—that the "I" is a legion of devils. Yes, the "I" exists in a pluralized manner. The five cylinders of the human machine originate and empower all of those little legions of "I's" that in their conjunction constitute that which is called ego, the "I," the self-willed. The pluralized "I" clumsily squanders the Essence that we carry within, which we need in order to build Soul. So, when we dissolve the pluralized "I" then the squanderer is terminated, the Essence is accumulated within us, and becomes a permanent center of gravity. When we establish within ourselves a permanent center of gravity, then sex works with its own energy, with its own Hydrogen, the Hydrogen Ti-12. Gnostic esotericism teaches that when the sexual center works with its own energy, with its own Hydrogen, then abuse of sex ceases, because then each center works with the energy that corresponds to it, with the Hydrogen that corresponds to it, and not with the Hydrogen Ti-12 stolen from sex.

If we want to end the abuse of sex, then it is necessary to dissolve the "I." In the past, many initiates partially dissolved the "I" and thanks to this they were able to build the superior, existential bodies of the Being. Regrettably, they soon forgot the necessity of totally disintegrating their "I" in a radical manner. The outcome of that negligence was a renewed strengthening of their pluralized "I." Those types of initiates were transformed into Hanasmussen with a "double center of gravity." In the internal worlds, these types of subjects have a double personality: one white and the other black. For example: Andrameleck. When we invoke this magician in the Molecular World, either a great Adept from the White Lodge or a great Adept from the Black Lodge can attend our call; they are two Adepts, and nevertheless one, same individual. Andrameleck is a Hanasmuss with double center of gravity; he is simultaneously a black and a white magician.

Whosoever does not want to truly suffer the horrible fate of Andrameleck has to intensely work with the three basic factors of the revolution of the consciousness. Whosoever wants to become liberated from the 48 laws must finish with the abuse of sex. Whosoever wants to finish with the abuse of sex must annihilate the "I," reduce it to dust. It is urgent to establish a complete equilibrium of all five centers of the human machine, and this is only possible by dissolving the "I."

Chapter 9

The "I" and the Being

In regards to psychological subject-matter, we must make a precise differentiation between the "I" and the Being. The "I" is not the Being, nor is the Being the "I." Regardless, everybody says, "my Being." Everybody thinks about their Being, yet no one knows what the Being is, thus they end up mistaking the Being for the "I."

When we knock at a door, if somebody questions us saying, "Who is it?," we always answer saying, "It is 'I'." In this we do not commit an error as the answer is exact. But when we say, "My entire being is sad, ill, tired, etc.," then indeed, we torpidly err because the wretched intellectual animal falsely called "human being" still does not possess the Being.

Only the Being can do, yet the human machine, the wretched intellectual animal, is not capable of doing anything; everything happens to him. He is a simple mechanical toy moved by forces that he does not know. The intellectual animal has the delusion of doing something, but indeed he does nothing: everything happens through him. They beat us and we react by beating. They harass us to pay the rent for the house, then we react anxiously looking for money. Somebody hurts our self-esteem, then we react by committing madness, etc.

The wretched intellectual animal is always a victim of circumstances and is not capable of consciously originating circumstances; but he wrongly believes that he actually originates them. Indeed, only the Being (the Innermost) can consciously determine circumstances; yet regrettably, the intellectual animal falsely called "human being" still does not possess the Being (the Innermost).

Many students from pseudo-occult, pseudo-esoteric schools, full of refined metaphysical ambitions, commit the error of dividing their beloved "I" into two arbitrary and absurd halves. They qualify the first half as Superior "I," and they contemptuously watch the second half, saying, "That is the Inferior 'I'." What is most intriguing of all of this—what is simultaneously the most comical and tragic—is to see that wretched Inferior "I" desperately fighting to evolve and perfect himself in order to someday achieve the longed for union with the Superior "I."

The wretched mind of the intellectual animal is ludicrous when fabricating the Superior "I," when conferring divine attributes onto it, when giving it arbitrary powers in order to control the mind and the heart. The same "I" divides itself into two. The same "I" wants to amalgamate itself after having divided itself into two. The same "I" splits and wants to join again. The ambitions of the "I" have no limits. It wants and wishes to become a Master, Deva, God, etc.

The "I" splits itself into two in order to join again and become one. Thus, this is how the "I" mistakenly believes that it can see its super-divine ambitions fulfilled. All of these tricks of the "I" are fine deceits of the mind, trivialities without any value whatsoever. The mind fabricates the comical Superior "I" to its taste, dresses it like a Mahatma, names it with a sonorous name, and thereafter exalts itself, falling into mythomania.

We knew the case of a mythomaniac that let his beard and hair grow long, then he dressed in a Jesus-type of Christian robe and told the whole world that he was no less than the very reincarnation of Jesus Christ. Naturally, there were many imbeciles who not only worshiped him but who still continue to worship him.

When having the bad taste of fabricating the Superior "I" as a separated and super-divine entity, the mind falsifies reality, mistakenly supposing such an entity is the Being, the Innermost, the Reality. The mind arbitrarily wants that Superior "I"—fabricated by itself—to be the Being. Thus, the mind stupidly grants to that Superior "I" things fabricated by itself, things that have nothing to do with the Being. These trivialities of the mind are similar to the falsification of currencies: the mind falsifies a false Being and that counterfeit bill is the Superior "I." Mythomaniacs have a terrible and frightful self-esteem. They live very attached to themselves. They worship their false coin, their so-boasted Superior "I."

Every mythomaniac is a ludicrous psychopath. Every mythomaniac overestimates himself excessively and considers himself to be a God that people are obligated to worship. Nevertheless, not all of those who fabricate a Superior "I"

fall into mythomania. Fanatics abound
who are not mythomaniacs, and who only
aspire to evolve in order to attain union
with their Superior "I." Those fanatics do
not eat a single piece of meat nor do they
drink a glass of wine, and they frightfully
criticize anyone who eats a tiny piece of
meat or who has a glass of wine in his
hand ready to make a toast. Those fanatics are unbearable. As a general rule they
are one hundred percent vegetarian; they
believe themselves to be very holy, even
when in their home they are cruel with
their spouse, their children, etc. Those
people love to fornicate, adulterate, covet,
lust; nonetheless, they believe they are
very holy.

The mind only serves as a hindrance
to the Being (the Innermost). The mind
does not know anything about Reality. If
thought knew Reality—the Innermost, the
Being—then all people would already be
comprehensive.

We can experience the Being, the
Innermost, only through profound
meditation. The experience of the Being,
the Innermost, transforms us radically. Outrageously, the mythomaniacs
usually falsify such an experience with

unconscious, mental self-projections
that they rush to tell the whole world.
Mythomaniacs are usually victims of self-
deceit, thus, believing themselves to be
Gods. They long for the whole world to
worship them.

It is completely impossible to experience the Being—the Innermost, the
Reality—without becoming true technical
and scientific masters of that mysterious
science called meditation. It is completely
impossible to experience the Being—the
Innermost, the Reality—without having
reached a true mastery of the quietude
and silence of the mind. Nevertheless, we
must not deceive ourselves and be ready
to buy a "pig in a poke," since the "I" also
lusts for and covets those silences, and it
even fabricates them artificially.

We need calm and total silence of
the mind during profound meditation.
Nonetheless, we do not need that false
quietude and silence fabricated by the "I."
Listen, we must not forget that when the
devil celebrates Mass, with his sermon he
deceives even the most astute people.

It is logical to state that if we are
moved by the greed of experiencing the
Being, and we want to silence the mind

by force, on a whim, if we want to calm
it by torturing it and fastening it, then
we will only obtain artificial silences
and arbitrary quietude produced by the
"I." Whosoever truly wants a legitimate
silence and not a false silence, a true quietude and not a false quietude, must be
integral—that is, to not commit the error
of dividing himself between subject and
object, thinker and thought, "I" and not
"I," controller and controlled, Superior "I"
and Inferior "I," me and my thoughts, etc.

To know how to meditate is to be on
the path of inner illumination. If we
want to learn how to meditate, we must
comprehend that between me and my
thoughts—in other words, between thinker and thought—there is no difference
whatsoever.

The human mind is not the brain. The
brain is made to elaborate thought, but it
is not thought. The mind is energetic and
subtle, but we commit the error of dividing ourselves into thousands of small
mental fragments, which in their conjunction compose that which is the legion of
the pluralized "I."

During meditation, when we try to
unite all of those mental fragments with

the healthy purpose of becoming integral, then all of those fragments form another great fragment against which we must fight. Here then, the quietude and silence of the mind becomes impossible. Therefore, during meditation we must not divide ourselves between Superior "I" and Inferior "I," me and my thoughts, my mind and "I" because the mind and "I," my thoughts and "I" are all one: the ego, the pluralized "I," the self-willed, etc.

When we truly comprehend that the Superior "I" and Inferior "I," as well as my thoughts and "I," etc. are all the ego, the self-willed, it is clear that by means of basic comprehension we liberate ourselves from dualistic thought. Thus, the mind is then truly quiet and in a profound silence. Only when the mind is really quiet, only when the mind is in a true silence can we then experience that which is the Reality, that which is the authentic Being, the Innermost.

It is totally impossible to become integral while the mind is bottled within dualism. The Essence of the mind (the Buddhata) is most precious, but regrettably it is bottled in the battle of antitheses. During meditation, when the Essence of the mind escapes from the bottle of the opposites, we can then experience the Reality, the Being, the Innermost.

There is dualism when I try to reunite all the fragments of my mind in one. There is dualism when my mind is enslaved by good and evil, cold and heat, big and small, pleasant and unpleasant, yes and no, etc. There is also dualism when we divide ourselves between Superior "I" and Inferior "I" and when we yearn for the Superior "I" to control us during meditation.

Whosoever has experienced the Being at some time during meditation is cured forever of the danger of falling into mythomania. The Being—the Innermost, the Reality—is totally different from that which the pseudo-occultists and pseudo-esotericists call Superior "I" or Divine "I."

The experience of Reality is completely different, distinct from everything the mind has ever experienced. The experience of Reality cannot be communicated to anybody because it does not look like anything that the mind has experienced before. When one has experienced Reality, one then comprehends very deeply the disastrous state in which one is abiding, and then one only aspires to know oneself without wanting to become more than one is.

At the present time, the wretched intellectual animal falsely called "human being" only has inside one useful element. This element is the Buddhata, the Essence of the mind, with which we can experience the Being, the Innermost, the Reality. This precious element is trapped in the bottle of the animal intellect. During profound inner meditation, when the mind is totally quiet and in an absolute silence— within and without, not only in the superficial level, but also in all the different corridors, subconscious extracts, zones and lands—then the Essence, the precious element, escapes from within the bottle and fuses with the Being, the Innermost, in order to experience Reality.

Chapter 10

The Truth

Many people believe in God, and many people are atheistic; they do not believe in God. There are also many individuals who neither believe nor do not believe, and try to behave well in life just in case there is God.

We state that a belief in God does not indicate experience of the Truth, That which is called God. We state that to deny God does not indicate experience of That which is the Truth, That which is called God. We state that doubt of the existence of God does not indicate experience of the Truth. We need to experience That, which can transform us radically—That, which many call God, Allah, Tao, Zen, Brahman, INRI, etc.

The mind of believers is bottled in beliefs. To believe is not an experience of That which is the Truth, God, Allah or whatever you want to call it. The mind of the atheist is bottled within incredulity, and is not the experience of the Truth, God, Brahman, etc. The mind of the one who doubts the existence of God is bottled in skepticism, and this is not the Truth. That which is, That which is the Truth—God, Allah, or whatever we want to call That which does not have a name—is totally different from any belief, negation, or skepticism. While the mind remains bottled within anyone of these three factors of ignorance, it cannot experience That which the Chinese call the Tao, That which is Divine, That which is the Truth, God, Allah, Brahma, etc. Whosoever has experienced That which some call God, That which cannot be defined—because if it is defined it is disfigured—it is clear that such a one undergoes a radical, total, and definitive transformation.

When Pilate asked Jesus, "What is the Truth?" Jesus kept silence. When the same question was asked to Buddha, he turned his back and walked away. The Truth is incommunicable, as incommunicable is the sublime ecstasy that we feel when we contemplate a beautiful sunset. The Truth is a matter of mystical experience. Thus, only by means of ecstasy can we experience it.

Everybody can give themselves the luxury of having an opinion about Truth; but Truth has nothing to do with opinions. Truth has nothing to do with thought. The Truth is something that we can only experience while in the absence of the "I."

The Truth comes to us as thief in the night, when it is not expected. Indeed, the Truth is something very paradoxical. The one who knows it does not say it, and the one who says it does not know it.

The Truth is not something quiet and static. The Truth is the unknowable, from moment to moment.

The Truth is not a goal where we must arrive.

The Truth is hidden within the depth of each problem of daily life.

The Truth does not belong to time, nor to eternity. The Truth is beyond time and eternity.

The Truth—God, Allah, Brahman, or whatever you want to call That which is the great Reality—is a series of always expansive and successively more and more deeply significant experiences.

Some people have an idea about the Truth, and other people have other ideas about it. Thus, everyone has their own ideas about the Truth; but the Truth has nothing to do with ideas. The Truth is totally different from all ideas. Hence, there are many people in the world who believe they have the Truth, without ever having experienced the Truth in their lives. Commonly, those people want to teach the Truth to those who indeed have once experienced it.

Without wise concentration of thought, the experience of the Truth is impossible.

There are two types of concentration: the first is the exclusive type of concentration. The second is the total, complete type; it is non-exclusive.

True concentration is not the outcome of options, with all of its fights; nor is it the outcome of the choosing of these or those thoughts: "that which I think," that this thought is good and that one is bad, and vice versa; "that which I must not think" about this and that; "it is better to think about that," etc. In fact, this forms conflicts between attention and distraction. Quietude and silence of the mind cannot exist where there are conflicts.

We must learn to wisely meditate, and as each thought, memory, image, idea, concept, etc., arises within the mind, we must watch it, study it, and extract what is of value from each thought, memory, image, etc.

When the parade of thoughts is exhausted, the mind remains quiet and in a profound silence. Then the Essence of the mind escapes, and the experience of That which is the Truth comes to us.

Our system of concentration excludes nothing; it is total, integral, complete. Our system of concentration includes everything and does not exclude anything. Our system of concentration is the way that leads us to the experience of the Truth.

Jesus Teaching Psychology

"Woe unto you, scribes [intellectuals] and Pharisees [believers], hypocrites! for ye make clean the outside of the cup and of the platter, but within they are full of extortion and excess. [Thou] blind Pharisee, cleanse first that [which is] within the cup and platter, that the outside of them may be clean also. Woe unto you, scribes and Pharisees, hypocrites! for ye are like unto whited sepulchres, which indeed appear beautiful outward, but are within full of dead [men's] bones, and of all uncleanness. Even so ye also outwardly appear righteous unto men, but within ye are full of hypocrisy and iniquity." - Jesus, from Matthew 23

Chapter 11

The Hidden Levels of the Subconsciousness

Not long ago, on a certain autumn night, a Gnostic student said to his Master, "I am no longer interested in attaining the realization of my Self, nor to perfect myself. The only thing I am interested in is to work for the liberation of the proletariat. Apart from that... to the Devil with all of us."

The Master responded, "Water and soap do not harm anybody. You can continue working for the proletariat, but wash yourself well, with a lot of soap." The student understood the parable of the Master and kept a respectful silence.

There are people who clean the outside of themselves—they do not eat meat, they do not drink, they do not smoke, they boast of being chaste—but they have wet dreams at night.

There are people who covet to not be covetous; those people detest covetousness, and nevertheless they covet to not be covetous. There are many people who covet virtues; their "I" is enchanted with medals, with being honored, with virtues. Wretched people, they think that by coveting virtues they will come to possess virtues.

People do not want to realize there is no love, and that only by comprehending all the processes of hatred in the different corridors, lands, and regions of the subconsciousness, then hatred ends and that which is called love is born in a natural and pure, spontaneous manner. Thus, this is how love comes into existence.

People covet the virtue of altruism, yet only by very thoroughly comprehending how egotism is processed in the different levels of the subconsciousness can we then annihilate egotism. Once egotism is dead, then without effort the precious flower of altruism is born within us.

People covet the precious virtue of humility, yet those wretched people do not want to comprehend that humility is a very exotic flower. Listen: the simple fact of feeling satisfied with having that virtue is enough for it to cease to exist within us. Hence, it is necessary to very thoroughly comprehend the process of pride in the different hidden levels of the subconsciousness. This is how pride ends, and then, without effort, the exotic flower of humility is born within us.

People covet the virtue of chastity. Yet, only by transmuting and sublimating the sexual energy, and only by comprehending all the processes of lust in all the hidden levels of the subconsciousness is this horrible vice annihilated and the exotic flower of chastity is born within us in a natural and sublime manner.

People covet the virtue of amiability. Yet only by comprehending all the processes of anger in the subconscious corridors of the mind can the precious virtue of amiability be born within us.

People covet the virtue of diligence. Yet only by integrally comprehending the processes of laziness in all the hidden levels of the subconsciousness can diligence be born within us, after laziness has been disintegrated.

Envy is the secret trigger of action in this society that is praised for being "civilized." There are people who covet the virtue of happiness for the success of others. However, only by comprehending that envy is unhappiness for the success of others, and that such a grief is processed in all the subconscious departments of the mind, can that grief be disintegrated. Then that is how happiness for the success of others is born within us.

Many people covet to not be gluttonous. Yet only by comprehending all the subconscious processes of gluttony can we then stop being gluttonous.

Gnostic students must learn how to explore the subconsciousness by means of meditation. To intellectually comprehend a defect is not enough. It is necessary to study the subconsciousness.

Often, a defect disappears from the surface of the intellect; however, it continues to exist in the different subconscious areas of the mind.

We need to die from moment to moment. As the defects are annihilated, accordingly the "I" dies from moment to moment. The "I" covets virtues in order to become strong. Do not covet virtues; virtues are born within us in the measure that our defects die, in accordance to the disintegration of the "I."

Only with a quiet and silent mind, submerged in profound inner meditation can we extract from within the tomb of the subconscious memory all the mil-

lenarian rottenness that we carry within
from ancient times. The subconsciousness is memory; the subconsciousness is
the black grave—pretty on the outside, yet
filthy on the inside. It is not pleasant to
see the black grave of the subconsciousness with all the bones and rottenness of
the past. Within the black, subconscious
grave, each hidden defect smells awful,
yet when seeing it, it is easy to burn it and
to reduce it to ashes. This is how we die
from moment to moment. It is necessary
to remove from within the tomb of our
memory all of that subconscious rottenness. Thus, only with quietude and mental silence can we extract from the black
subconscious grave all the rottenness of
the past, in order to reduce it to ashes
with the wonderful fire, with profound
comprehension.

When many Gnostic students explore
the subconsciousness, they commit the
error of dividing themselves between
intellect and subconsciousness, analyzer
and analyzed, subject and object, perceiver
and perceived, I and my subconsciousness, etc. These types of divisions create
antagonisms, fights, battles between
that which I am and that which is the

subconsciousness, between intellect and subconsciousness. Those types of fights are absurd because I and my subconsciousness is all "I," all subconscious "I." Intellect and subconsciousness are all subconsciousness, because the intellect is also subconsciousness. The intellectual animal is ninety-seven percent subconscious. The human machine has not awakened consciousness yet. For that reason it is solely a human machine.

When the mind is divided between intellect and subconsciousness, analyzer and analyzed, etc., there are antagonisms and fights, and where there are antagonisms and fights then there is no quietude and silence of the mind. Only with perfect quietude and mental silence can we extract from the black, subconscious, mental grave all the rottenness of the past, in order to burn it and reduce it to dust with the fire of comprehension. Let us not state, "My "I" has anger, greed, lust, pride, laziness, gluttony, etc." It is better to state, "I have anger, greed, etc."

Chapter 12

The Chinese Master
Han Shan

A summary of the autobiography of the Chinese Master named Han Shan has arrived to us, which is worth commenting on for the best comprehension of this 1965-1966 Christmas Message.

The Master Han Shan was born in Chuan Chia, in the beautiful Chinese region of Nanking. In dreams, the Divine Mother announced to a very humble woman from that region that she would conceive a child, and indeed she conceived a beautiful child that was born the 12th of October of 1545. That child was the great Chinese Master named Han Shan.

When the child was a few years old, he caught a very critical sickness that nearly killed him. His humble mother, filled with faith, prayed to the Divine Mother Kundalini (Guanyin), promising Her with all of her heart that if the child recovered she would place him in a monastery and allow him to become a monk. Thus, when the child recovered, his beloved mother registered his name ("Heshang," Buddhist monk) at the Longevity Buddhist Monastery.

From a very early age, the child Han Shan demonstrated to truly be a Master. When an uncle of the boy died and another aunt gave birth to a child, Han Shan worried intensely about studying the mysteries of life and death.

Han Shan's mother was really very severe with the boy. On a certain occasion she said, "I must overcome his very tender nature so that he will study as he should, otherwise he will be useless."

At the appropriate age the boy entered the monastery and became a true devotee of Guanyin, the Divine Mother. On a given moment, he recited the entire Sutra of the Bodhisattva Guanyin for his beloved mother, and naturally she was astonished and delighted.

Tradition states that when the Master Da Zhou Zhao saw this beautiful boy, he joyfully exclaimed, "This boy will be a Master of men and of heavens." When that Master asked the boy, "Which would you rather be: an official or a Buddha?" the boy answered with complete certainty, "I want to be a Buddha."

As a youngster, Han Shan became deeply preoccupied in the pursuit of his esoteric calling. After reading a copy of the sayings of the life of the great Chinese Master Zhong Feng, he dedicated himself to his spiritual life. Tradition states that Amitabha Buddha, Kwan Yin, and Mahasthamaprapta (Dashizhi) appeared to him in the internal worlds. Undoubtedly, all of this was definitive in order for Han Shan to fully dedicate himself to his esoteric life.

After listening to a marvelous lecture about "The Ten Wondrous Gateways of the Ocean Symbol Samadhi," Han Shan adopted the name "Cheng Yin."

When Cheng Yin was twenty years old, the Abbot Master—his great Master—died. However, before dying, the Abbot Master gathered all his disciples together and said, "I am eighty-three years old and soon will leave this Earth. Though I have over eighty disciples, none of them will be able to take my place..." The Abbot Master then said, "I wish Han Shan (Cheng Yin) to continue my work. Yes, although he is young, he is as able as an adult. After my death, despite his youth, you will have to respect his word." Thus, this is how the

Chinese Master Han Shan began his great work in this world.

When studying the concepts of the book by Zhao Lun and preparing it for printing, he became enlightened when reading the section that contained a story about a Brahmin who went back to visit the home he had left as a child. Though the Brahmin's hair was white and he had aged considerably, the neighbors were able to recognize him and exclaimed, "Look, the man who used to live here is still alive." Yet the old Brahmin smiled and said: "Oh, no. I look like an old man, but in reality I am not." When Han Shan read this, he said, "Only appearances change. The underlying Dharma does not have a beginning or end!" How truthful this is, how truthful!

The Chan Master Fa Guang was the one who instructed Han Shan profoundly about the scientific technique of meditation. He taught Han Shan about the disassociation of the mind, the subconsciousness, sensorial perceptions, and how to maintain himself beyond the dualities of sacredness and profanity, or saintly and worldly knowledge during meditation.

The associations of the mind that form phrases, memories, images, ideas, desires, etc., constitute the fundamental cause of that incessant mental chatter and the entire battle of the antitheses. If based in comprehension we attain mental disassociation—if based in comprehension we obtain the disassociation of all subconscious memories—if based in comprehension we manage to eliminate the subjective elements of our perceptions, then it is clear that the mind remains quiet and in silence, not only in the superficial level, but also in the most profound levels of the subconsciousness.

Han Shan attained the quietude and silence of the mind. He became in fact an enlightened Master of Perfection. Ancient wise men said, "Whosoever does not allow his mind to become disturbed when hearing the sound of running water for thirty years will soon attain the all-pervading wisdom of the miraculous Bodhisattva Avalokiteshvara."

Han Shan became an athlete of internal meditation, thus nothing could disturb him. His food consisted of grains, vegetables, and rice, just enough to live.

Han Shan became a true athlete of the quietude and silence of the mind. Thus, it is clear that he achieved enlightenment.

The powers that many covet are the outcome or consequence of enlightenment. Yes, when we have really arrived at enlightenment, then powers come to the mystic without the need to covet them.

Han Shan said, "Everyday I cooked rice and ate it with wild vegetables and porridge. Then, after the meal, I would take a nice walk. But while I was walking one day, I happened to stop and stand still, noticing that I have neither body nor mind. In that blissful moment, I entered samadhi. Soon I ceased to be aware of anything except a great omnipresent, perfect, lucid, and serene brightness, round and full, clean and still like a huge round mirror." From then, all of the powers of positive clairvoyance, formidable clairaudience, telepathy, regal intuition, etc., awoke totally in Han Shan, thanks to the quietude and silence of the mind, and as a consequence of enlightenment.

Han Shan composed the following precious poem, transcribed by Chan Chen Chi:

"In utter stillness, the bright light,
pervading all, enfolds the great void.
"When closely looked at, worldly
things are like illusions in a dream.
"Today I really comprehended that
the Buddha's words are just and
true!"

Based on very intimate meditation and
on the supreme quietude and silence of
the mind, Han Shan managed to awaken
the Buddhata—that is to say, the Essence,
the consciousness. During the hours of
sleep, Han Shan stopped dreaming and
lived totally awake within the superior
worlds. When returning to his physical
body after the rest of sleep, he brought to
his physical brain all the memories of his
experiences within the superior worlds.
Han Shan attained all of that based on
mental quietude and silence.

One night while his physical body slept,
Han Shan entered the great temple of wisdom. The great Masters Qing Liang and
Miao Feng—in their astral bodies—wel-
comed him with immense joy. In that sol-
emn temple, Han Shan received the most
precious teaching regarding the entrance
into the state of the Dharmadhatu, in
which he learned in depth about the laws

of evolution or progress and devolution or retrogress.

Han Shan also comprehended that there are Buddhic lands that penetrate and co-penetrate each other without being confused, and that in those lands excellence and service are fundamental. He comprehended that in us what discriminates is the subconsciousness, and what does not discriminate is wisdom. He also comprehended that purity or impurity depend totally upon our mind.

In his astral body in the temple of Maitreya Bodhisattva, Han Shan opened and read in a sutra,

> "Discrimination [vikalpa] is subconsciousness. Nondiscrimination [nirvikalpa jnana] is wisdom. Clinging to subconsciousness will bring corruption, but clinging to wisdom will bring purity. Corruption leads to birth and death, but purity leads to Nirvana. If one attains purity, then there is no need for Buddhas."

When after many long years of absence Han Shan returned to his house, the neighbors asked his mother, "Where did he come from? Did he come by boat or by land?" His mother replied, "Well, he came from the void!"

Certainly, Han Shan came from the Illuminating Void. Thus, this is how it is written and how Chang Chen Chi narrated it.

After great practices, the quietude and absolute silence of the mind brings about the bursting of the bag, our entrance into the Illuminating Void. We then enter into ecstasy, because our consciousness awakens.

Final Salutations

With immense love I send my fervent greeting for Christmas and New Year 1965-1966 to all the Gnostic brothers and sisters of the entire world. It is necessary that all of you, my brothers and sisters, comprehend that we are delivering the second part of our message.

Study, beloved ones. Practice meditation in all the Lumisials and also individually. The Gnostic Lumisials must become centers of meditation. Practice, most beloved ones. Pray. Transmute your sexual secretions in light and fire. Dissolve the "I." Fight unceasingly everywhere for the opening of more and more Lumisials. You have to establish regulations in them, yet amongst those regulations you must include at least one hour of group meditation. Remember that group meditation forms a formidable magnetic vortex that by cosmic magnetization has the power to attract towards you certain divine types of very necessary forces. Every Lumisial must be a meditation center. Thus, multiply the Lumisials everywhere for the good of the Great

Work of the Father. It is urgent for all Lumisials to have missionaries so that they can work with extreme intensity for the opening of more and more Lumisials everywhere.

Most beloved ones, receive my Gnostic greeting: inverential peace. May the star of Bethlehem shine on your path. With all of my heart I wish you a happy Christmas and a prosperous New Year.

Glossary

Absolute: Abstract space; that which is without attributes or limitations. The Absolute has three aspects: the Ain, the Ain Soph, and the Ain Soph Aur.

"The Absolute is the Being of all Beings. The Absolute is that which Is, which always has Been, and which always will Be. The Absolute is expressed as Absolute Abstract Movement and Repose. The Absolute is the cause of Spirit and of Matter, but It is neither Spirit nor Matter. The Absolute is beyond the mind; the mind cannot understand It. Therefore, we have to intuitively understand Its nature." - Samael Aun Weor, *Tarot and Kabbalah*

"In the Absolute we go beyond karma and the gods, beyond the law. The mind and the individual consciousness are only good for mortifying our lives. In the Absolute we do not have an individual mind or individual consciousness; there, we are the unconditioned, free and absolutely happy Being. The Absolute is life free in its movement, without conditions, limitless, without the mortifying fear of the law, life beyond spirit and matter, beyond karma and suffering, beyond thought, word and action, beyond silence and sound, beyond forms."
- Samael Aun Weor, *The Major Mysteries*

Akashic Records: Permanent impressions held in nature of everything that has ever occured, i.e. "the memory of nature." By means of awakening consciousness, it is possible to access past, present, and future events within these records.

Astral: This term is derived from "pertaining to or proceeding from the stars," but in the esoteric knowledge it refers to the emotional aspect of the fifth dimension, which in Hebrew is called Hod.

Astral Body: What is commonly called the Astral Body is not the true Astral Body, it is rather the Lunar Protoplasmatic Body, also known as the Kama Rupa (Sanskrit, "body of desires") or "dream body" (Tibetan rmi-lam-gyi lus). The true Astral Body is Solar (being superior to Lunar Nature) and must be created, as the Master Jesus indicated in the Gospel of John 3:5-6, "Except a man be born of water and of the Spirit, he cannot enter into the kingdom of God. That which is born of the flesh is flesh; and that which is born of the Spirit is spirit." The Solar Astral Body is created as a result of the Third Initiation of Major Mysteries (Serpents of Fire), and is perfected in the Third Serpent of Light. In Tibetan Buddhism, the Solar Astral Body is known as the illusory body (sgyu-lus). This body is related to the emotional center and to the sephirah Hod.

"Really, only those who have worked with the Maithuna (White Tantra) for many years can possess the Astral Body." - Samael Aun Weor, *The Elimination of Satan's Tail*

Buddhata: Derived from "buddhadatu" (Sanskrit), which means "essence of the Buddha," referring to the Buddha Nature or seed. This is the consciousness, the embryo of soul, also known as the Essence or Tathagatagarbha.

Centers, Seven: The human being has seven centers of psychological activity. The first five are the Intellectual, Emotional, Motor, Instinctive, and Sexual Centers. However, through inner development one learns how to utilize the Superior Emotional and Superior Intellectual Centers. Most people do not use these two at all.

Christ: Derived from the Greek Christos, "the Anointed One," and Krestos, whose esoteric meaning is "fire." The word Christ is a title, not a personal name.

"Indeed, Christ is a Sephirothic Crown (Kether, Chokmah and Binah) of incommensurable wisdom, whose purest atoms shine within Chokmah, the world of the Ophanim. Christ is not the Monad, Christ is not the Theosophical Septenary; Christ is not the Jivan-Atman. Christ is the Central Sun. Christ is the ray that unites us to the Absolute." - Samael Aun Weor, *Tarot and Kabbalah*

"The Gnostic Church adores the Saviour of the World, Jesus. The Gnostic Church knows that Jesus incarnated Christ, and that is why they adore him. Christ is not a human nor a divine individual. Christ is a title given to all fully self-realised Masters. Christ is the Army of the Voice. Christ is the Verb. The Verb is far beyond the body, the soul and the Spirit. Everyone who is able to incarnate the Verb receives in fact the title of Christ. Christ is the Verb itself. It is necessary for everyone of us to incarnate the

Verb (Word). When the Verb becomes flesh in us we speak with the verb of light. In actuality, several Masters have incarnated the Christ. In secret India, the Christ Yogi Babaji has lived for millions of years; Babaji is immortal. The Great Master of Wisdom Kout Humi also incarnated the Christ. Sanat Kumara, the founder of the Great College of Initiates of the White Lodge, is another living Christ. In the past, many incarnated the Christ. In the present, some have incarnated the Christ. In the future many will incarnate the Christ. John the Baptist also incarnated the Christ. John the Baptist is a living Christ. The difference between Jesus and the other Masters that also incarnated the Christ has to do with Hierarchy. Jesus is the highest Solar Initiate of the Cosmos..." - Samael Aun Weor, *The Perfect Matrimony*

Consciousness: "Wherever there is life, there exists the consciousness. Consciousness is inherent to life as humidity is inherent to water." - Samael Aun Weor, *Fundamental Notions of Endocrinology and Criminology*

From various dictionaries: 1. The state of being conscious; knowledge of one's own existence, condition, sensations, mental operations, acts, etc. 2. Immediate knowledge or perception of the presence of any object, state, or sensation. 3. An alert cognitive state in which you are aware of yourself and your situation. In Universal Gnosticism, the range of potential consciousness is allegorized in the Ladder of Jacob, upon which the angels ascend and descend. Thus there are higher and lower levels of consciousness, from the level of demons at the bottom, to highly realized angels in the heights.

"It is vital to understand and develop the conviction that consciousness has the potential to increase to an infinite degree." - The 14th Dalai Lama.

"Light and consciousness are two phenomena of the same thing; to a lesser degree of consciousness, corresponds a lesser degree of light; to a greater degree of consciousness, a greater degree of light." - Samael Aun Weor, *The Esoteric Treatise of Hermetic Astrology*

Cosmocreator: An awakened cosmic intelligence capable of creating a planet or sun. An Elohim.

Divine Mother: "Among the Aztecs, she was known as Tonantzin, among the Greeks as chaste Diana. In Egypt she was Isis, the Divine Mother, whose veil no mortal has lifted. There is no doubt at all that esoteric Christianity has never forsaken the worship of the Divine Mother Kundalini. Obviously she is Marah, or better said, RAM-IO, MARY. What orthodox religions did not specify, at least with regard to the exoteric or public circle, is the aspect of Isis in her individual human form. Clearly, it was taught only in secret to the Initiates that this Divine Mother exists individually within each human being. It cannot be emphasized enough that Mother-God, Rhea, Cybele, Adonia, or whatever we wish to call her, is a variant of our own individual Being in the here and now. Stated explicitly, each of us has our own particular, individual Divine Mother." - Samael Aun Weor, *The Great Rebellion*

"Devi Kundalini, the Consecrated Queen of Shiva, our personal Divine Cosmic Individual Mother, assumes five transcendental mystic aspects in every creature, which we must enumerate:

1. The unmanifested Prakriti

2. The chaste Diana, Isis, Tonantzin, Maria or better said Ram-Io

3. The terrible Hecate, Persephone, Coatlicue, queen of the infernos and death; terror of love and law

4. The special individual Mother Nature, creator and architect of our physical organism

5. The Elemental Enchantress to whom we owe every vital impulse, every instinct." - Samael Aun Weor, *The Mystery of the Golden Blossom*

Ego: The multiplicity of contradictory psychological elements that we have inside are in their sum the "ego." Each one is also called "an ego" or an "I." Every ego is a psychological defect which produces suffering. The ego is three (related to our Three Brains or three centers of psychological processing), seven (capital sins), and legion (in their infinite variations).

"The ego is the root of ignorance and pain." - Samael Aun Weor, *The Esoteric Treatise of Hermetic Astrology*

"The Being and the ego are incompatible. The Being and the ego are like water and oil. They can never be mixed... The annihilation of the psychic aggregates (egos) can be made possible only by radically comprehending our errors through meditation and by the evident Self-reflection of the Being." - Samael Aun Weor, *The Pistis Sophia Unveiled*

Ens Seminis: (Latin) Literally, "the entity of semen." A term used by Paracelsus.

Essence: "Without question the Essence, or Consciousness, which is the same thing, sleeps deeply... The Essence in itself is very beautiful. It came from above, from the stars. Lamentably, it is smothered deep within all these "I's" we carry inside. By contrast, the Essence can retrace its steps, return to the point of origin, go back to the stars, but first it must liberate itself from its evil companions, who have trapped it within the slums of perdition. Human beings have three percent free Essence, and the other ninety-seven percent is imprisoned within the "I's"." - Samael Aun Weor, *The Great Rebellion*

"A percentage of psychic Essence is liberated when a defect is disintegrated. Thus, the psychic Essence which is bottled up within our defects will be completely liberated when we disintegrate each and every one of our false values, in other words, our defects. Thus, the radical transformation of ourselves will occur when the totality of our Essence is liberated. Then, in that precise moment, the eternal values of the Being will express themselves through us. Unquestionably, this would be marvelous not only for us, but also for all of humanity." - Samael Aun Weor, *The Revolution of the Dialectic*

Fornication: Originally, the term fornication was derived from the Indo-European word gwher, whose meanings relate to heat and burning (the full explanation can be found online at http://sacred-sex.org/terminology/fornication). Fornication means to make the heat (solar fire) of the seed (sexual power) leave the body through voluntary orgasm. Any voluntary orgasm is fornication, whether between a married man and woman, or an unmarried man and woman, or through masturbation, or in any other case; this is explained by Moses: "A man from whom there is a discharge of semen, shall immerse all his flesh in water, and he shall remain unclean until evening. And any garment or any leather [object] which has semen on it, shall be immersed in water, and shall remain unclean until evening. A woman with whom a man cohabits, whereby there was [a discharge of] semen, they shall immerse in water, and they shall remain unclean until evening." - Leviticus 15:16-18

To fornicate is to spill the sexual energy through the orgasm. Those who "deny themselves" restrain the sexual energy, and "walk in the midst of the fire" without being burned. Those who restrain the sexual energy, who renounce the orgasm, remember God in themselves, and do not defile themselves with animal passion, "for the temple of God is holy, which temple ye are."

"Whosoever is born of God doth not commit sin; for his seed remaineth in him: and he cannot sin, because he is born of God." - 1 John 3:9

This is why neophytes always took a vow of sexual abstention, so that they could prepare themselves for marriage, in which they would

have sexual relations but not release the sexual
energy through the orgasm. This is why Paul
advised:

"...they that have wives be as though they had
none..." - I Corinthians 7:29

"A fornicator is an individual who has intensely
accustomed his genital organs to copulate (with
orgasm). Yet, if the same individual changes
his custom of copulation to the custom of no
copulation, then he transforms himself into
a chaste person. We have as an example the
astonishing case of Mary Magdalene, who was
a famous prostitute. Mary Magdalene became
the famous Saint Mary Magdalene, the repented
prostitute. Mary Magdalene became the chaste
disciple of Christ." - Samael Aun Weor, *The
Revolution of Beelzebub*

Gnosis: (Greek) Knowledge.

1. The word Gnosis refers to the knowledge we
acquire through our own experience, as opposed
to knowledge that we are told or believe in.
Gnosis - by whatever name in history or culture - is conscious, experiential knowledge, not
merely intellectual or conceptual knowledge,
belief, or theory. This term is synonymous with
the Hebrew "daath" and the Sanskrit "jna."

2. The tradition that embodies the core wisdom
or knowledge of humanity.

"Gnosis is the flame from which all religions
sprouted, because in its depth Gnosis is religion. The word "religion" comes from the Latin
word "religare," which implies "to link the Soul
to God"; so Gnosis is the very pure flame from

where all religions sprout, because Gnosis is Knowledge, Gnosis is Wisdom." - Samael Aun Weor, *The Esoteric Path*

"The secret science of the Sufis and of the Whirling Dervishes is within Gnosis. The secret doctrine of Buddhism and of Taoism is within Gnosis. The sacred magic of the Nordics is within Gnosis. The wisdom of Hermes, Buddha, Confucius, Mohammed and Quetzalcoatl, etc., etc., is within Gnosis. Gnosis is the Doctrine of Christ." - Samael Aun Weor, *The Revolution of Beelzebub*

Hanasmuss: (plural: Hanasmussen) A Middle Eastern term referring to a person with a divided consciousness: part of it is free and natural, and part is trapped in the ego. In synthesis, everyone who has ego is a Hanasmuss. Although there are many variations and kinds of Hanasmussen, Gnosis generally describes four primary grades:

· mortal: the common person

· those with the Solar Astral body

· those with the Solar Bodies created

· fallen Angels

These are described in detail by Samael Aun Weor in the lecture "The Master Key."

"The Twice-born who does not reduce his Lunar Ego to cosmic dust converts himself into an abortion of the Cosmic Mother. He becomes a Marut, and there exist thousands of types of Maruts. Certain oriental sects and some Muslim tribes commit the lamentable error of rendering cult to all of those families of Maruts. Every

Marut, every Hanasmuss (plural: Hanasmussen) has in fact two personalities: one White and another Black (one Solar and another Lunar). The Innermost, the Being dressed with the Solar Electronic Bodies, is the White Personality of the Hanasmuss, and the pluralized "I" dressed with the Protoplasmic Lunar Bodies is the Hanasmuss' Black Personality. Therefore, these Maruts have a double center of gravity." - Samael Aun Weor

Hydrogen: (from Hydro- water, Gen- generate, genes, genesis, etc.) Hydrogen is the simplest element on the periodic table, and in Gnosticism it is recognized as the element that is the building block of all forms of matter. Hydrogen is a packet of solar light. The solar light (the light that comes from the sun) is the reflection of the Okidanok, the Cosmic Christ, which creates and sustains every world. This element is the fecundated water, generated water (hydro). The water is the source of all life. Everything that we eat, breathe and all of the impressions that we receive are in the form of various structures of hydrogen. Samael Aun Weor will place a note (Do, Re, Mi...) and a number related with the vibration and atomic weight (level of complexity) with a particular hydrogen. For example, he constantly refers to the Hydrogen Si-12. "Si" is the highest note in the octave and it is the result of the notes that come before it. This particular hydrogen is always related to the forces of Yesod, which is the synthesis and coagulation of all food, air, and impressions that we have previously received. Food begins at Do-768, air begins at Do-384, and impressions begin at Do-48. For more understanding visit GnosticTeachings. org for chapters and lectures related to "The Pancatattva Ritual" and "The Transformation of Impressions."

Innermost: "Our real Being is of a universal nature. Our real Being is neither a kind of superior nor inferior "I." Our real Being is impersonal, universal, divine. He transcends every concept of "I," me, myself, ego, etc., etc." - Samael Aun Weor, The Perfect Matrimony

Also known as Atman, the Spirit, Chesed, our own individual interior divine Father.

"The Innermost is the ardent flame of Horeb. In accordance with Moses, the Innermost is the Ruach Elohim (the Spirit of God) who sowed the waters in the beginning of the world. He is the Sun King, our Divine Monad, the Alter-Ego of Cicerone." - Samael Aun Weor, *The Revolution of Beelzebub*

Intellectual Animal: When the Intelligent Principle, the Monad, sends its spark of consciousness into Nature, that spark, the anima, enters into manifestation as a simple mineral. Gradually, over millions of years, the anima gathers experience and evolves up the chain of life until it perfects itself in the level of the mineral kingdom. It then graduates into the plant kingdom, and subsequently into the animal kingdom. With each ascension the spark receives new capacities and higher grades of complexity. In the animal kingdom it learns procreation by ejaculation. When that animal intelligence enters into the human kingdom, it receives a new capacity: reasoning, the intellect; it is now an anima with intellect: an Intellectual Animal. That spark must then perfect itself in the human kingdom in order to become a complete and perfect Human Being, an entity that has conquered and transcended everything that belongs to the lower kingdoms. Unfortunately, very few Intellectual Animals perfect themselves; most remain enslaved by their animal nature, and thus are reabsorbed by Nature, a process belonging to the Devolving side of life and called by all the great religions "Hell" or the Second Death.

"The present manlike being is not yet human; he is merely an intellectual animal. It is a very grave error to call the legion of the "I" the "soul." In fact, what the manlike being has is the psychic material, the material for the soul within his Essence, but indeed, he does not have a Soul yet." - Samael Aun Weor, *The Revolution of the Dialectic*

Internal Worlds: The many dimensions beyond the physical world. These dimensions are both subjective and objective. To know the objective internal worlds (the Astral Plane, or Nirvana, or the Klipoth) one must first know one's own personal, subjective internal worlds, because the two are intimately associated.

"Whosoever truly wants to know the internal worlds of the planet Earth or of the solar system or of the galaxy in which we live, must previously know his intimate world, his individual, internal life, his own internal worlds.

Man, know thyself, and thou wilt know the Universe and its Gods. The more we explore this internal world called "myself," the more we will comprehend that we simultaneously live in two worlds, in two realities, in two confines: the external and the internal. In the same way that it is indispensable for one to learn how to walk in the external world so as not to fall down into a precipice, or not get lost in the streets of the city, or to select one's friends, or not associate with the perverse ones, or not eat poison, etc.; likewise, through the psychological work upon oneself we learn how to walk in the internal world, which is explorable only through Self-observation." - Samael Aun Weor, *Revolutionary Psychology*

Through the work in Self-observation, we develop the capacity to awaken where previously we were asleep: including in the objective internal worlds.

Kundalini: "Kundalini, the serpent power or mystic fire, is the primordial energy or Sakti that lies dormant or sleeping in the Muladhara Chakra, the centre of the body. It is called the serpentine or annular power on account of serpentine form. It is an electric fiery occult power, the great pristine force which underlies all organic and inorganic matter. Kundalini is the cosmic power in individual bodies. It is not a material force like electricity, magnetism, centripetal or centrifugal force. It is a spiritual potential Sakti or cosmic power. In reality it has no form. [...] O Divine Mother Kundalini, the Divine Cosmic Energy that is hidden in men! Thou art Kali, Durga, Adisakti, Rajarajeswari, Tripurasundari, Maha-Lakshmi, Maha-Sarasvati! Thou hast put on all these names and forms. Thou hast manifested as Prana, electricity, force, magnetism, cohesion, gravitation in this universe. This whole universe rests in Thy bosom. Crores of salutations unto thee. O Mother of this world! Lead me on to open the Sushumna Nadi and take Thee along the Chakras to Sahasrara Chakra and to merge myself in Thee and Thy consort, Lord Siva. Kundalini Yoga is that Yoga which treats of Kundalini Sakti, the six centres of spiritual energy (Shat Chakras), the arousing of the sleeping Kundalini Sakti and its union with Lord Siva in Sahasrara Chakra, at the crown of the head. This is an exact science. This is also known as Laya Yoga. The six centres are pierced (Chakra Bheda) by the passing of Kundalini Sakti to the top of the head. 'Kundala' means 'coiled'. Her form is like a coiled serpent. Hence the name Kundalini." - Swami Sivananda, *Kundalini Yoga*

Logos: (Greek) means Verb or Word. In Greek and Hebrew metaphysics, the unifying principle of the world. The Logos is the manifested deity of every nation and people; the outward expression or the effect of the cause which is ever concealed. (Speech is the "logos" of thought). The Logos has three aspects, known universally as the Trinity or Trimurti. The First Logos is the Father, Brahma. The Second Logos is the Son, Vishnu. The Third Logos is the Holy Spirit,

Shiva. One who incarnates the Logos becomes a Logos.

"The Logos is not an individual. The Logos is an army of ineffable beings." - Samael Aun Weor, *Fundamental Notions of Endocrinology and Criminology*

Magic: The word magic is derived from the ancient word "mag" that means priest. Real magic is the work of a priest. A real magician is a priest.

"Magic, according to Novalis, is the art of influencing the inner world consciously." - Samael Aun Weor, *The Mystery of the Golden Blossom*

"When magic is explained as it really is, it seems to make no sense to fanatical people. They prefer to follow their world of illusions." - Samael Aun Weor, *The Revolution of Beelzebub*

Maithuna: The Sanskrit word maithuna is used in Hindu Tantras (esoteric scriptures) to refer to the sacrament (sacred ritual) of sexual union between husband and wife.

Maithuna or Mithuna has various appearances in scripture:

· Mithuna: paired, forming a pair; copulation; the zodiacal sign of Gemini in Vedic Astrology, which is depicted as a man and woman in a sexual embrace

· Mithunaya: to unite sexually

· Mithuni: to become paired, couple or united sexually

By means of the original Tantric Maithuna, after being prepared psychologically and spiritually and initiated by a genuine teacher (guru), the couple learns how to utilize their love and spiritual aspiration in order to transform their natural sexual forces to purify the mind, eliminate psychological defects, and awaken the latent powers of the consciousness. The man represents Shiva, the masculine aspect of the creative divine, and the woman represents Shakti, the feminine aspect and the source of the power of creation. This method was kept in strictest secrecy for thousands of years in order to preserve it in its pure form, and to prevent crude-minded people from deviating the teaching, other people, or harming themselves. Nonetheless, some degenerated traditions (popularly called "left-hand" traditions, or black magic) interpret Maithuna or sacramental sexuality according to their state of degeneration, and use these sacred teachings to justify their lust, desire, orgies, and other types of deviations from pure, genuine Tantra.

Krishna: "And I am the strength of the strong, devoid of lust and attachment. O best of the Bharatas, I am sex not contrary to dharma." (Bhagavad Gita 7.11)

Mantra: (Sanskrit, literally "mind protection") A sacred word or sound. The use of sacred words and sounds is universal throughout all religions and mystical traditions, because the root of all creation is in the Great Breath or the Word, the Logos. "In the beginning was the Word..."

Master: Like many terms related to spirituality, this one is grossly misunderstood. Samael Aun Weor wrote while describing the Germanic Edda, "In this Genesis of creation we discover Sexual Alchemy. The Fire fecundated the cold waters of chaos. The masculine principle Alfadur fecundated the feminine principle Niffleheim, dominated by Surtur (the Darkness), to bring forth life. That is how Ymir is born, the father of the giants, the Internal God of every human being, the Master." Therefore, the Master is the Innermost, Atman, the Father.

"The only one who is truly great is the Spirit, the Innermost. We, the intellectual animals, are leaves that the wind tosses about... No student of occultism is a Master. True Masters are only those who have reached the Fifth Initiation of Major Mysteries. Before the Fifth Initiation nobody is a Master." - Samael Aun Weor, *The Perfect Matrimony*

Meditation: "When the esotericist submerges himself into meditation, what he seeks is information." - Samael Aun Weor

"It is urgent to know how to meditate in order to comprehend any psychic aggregate, or in other words, any psychological defect. It is indispensable to know how to work with all our heart and with all our soul, if we want the elimination to occur." - Samael Aun Weor, *The Pistis Sophia Unveiled*

"1. The Gnostic must first attain the ability to stop the course of his thoughts, the capacity to not think. Indeed, only the one who achieves that capacity will hear the Voice of the Silence.

"2. When the Gnostic disciple attains the capacity to not think, then he must learn to concentrate his thoughts on only one thing.

"3. The third step is correct meditation. This brings the first flashes of the new consciousness into the mind.

"4. The fourth step is contemplation, ecstasy or Samadhi. This is the state of Turiya (perfect clairvoyance). - Samael Aun Weor, *The Perfect Matrimony*

Nirvana: (Sanskrit, "extinction"; Tibetan: nyangde, literally "the state beyond sorrow") In general use, refers to the permanent cessation of suffering and its causes, and therefore refers to a state of consciousness rather than a place. Yet, the term can also apply to heavenly realms, whose vibration is directed related to the cessation of suffering. In other words, if your mind-stream has liberated itself from the causes of suffering, it will naturally vibrate at the level of Nirvana (heaven).

"When the Soul fuses with the Inner Master, then it becomes free from Nature and enters into the supreme happiness of absolute existence. This state of happiness is called Nirvana. Nirvana can be attained through millions of births and deaths, but it can also be attained by means of a shorter path; this is the path of "initiation." The Initiate can reach Nirvana in one single life if he so wants it." - Samael Aun Weor, *The Zodiacal Course*

Samadhi: (Sanskrit) Literally means "union" or "combination" and its Tibetan equivilent means "adhering to that which is profound and definitive," or ting nge dzin, meaning "To hold unwaveringly, so there is no movement." Related terms include satori, ecstasy, manteia, etc. Samadhi is a state of consciousness. In the west, the term is used to describe an ecstatic state of consciousness in which the Essence escapes the painful limitations of the mind (the "I") and therefore experiences what is real: the Being, the Great Reality. There are many levels of Samadhi. In the sutras and tantras the term Samadhi has a much broader application whose precise interpretation depends upon which school and teaching is using it.

"Ecstasy is not a nebulous state, but a transcendental state of wonderment, which is associated with perfect mental clarity." - Samael Aun Weor, *The Elimination of Satan's Tail*

Self-realization: The achievement of perfect knowledge. This phrase is better stated as, "The realization of the Innermost Self," or "The realization of the true nature of self." At the ultimate level, this is the experiential, conscious knowledge of the Absolute, which is synonymous with Emptiness, Shunyata, or Non-being.

Sexual Magic: The word magic is derived from the ancient word magos "one of the members of the learned and priestly class," from O.Pers. magush, possibly from PIE *magh- "to be able, to have power." [Quoted from Online Etymology Dictionary].

"All of us possess some electrical and magnetic forces within, and, just like a magnet, we exert a force of attraction and repulsion... Between

lovers that magnetic force is particularly power-
ful and its action has a far-reaching effect."
- Samael Aun Weor, *The Mystery of the Golden
Blossom*

Sexual magic refers to an ancient science that
has been known and protected by the purest,
most spiritually advanced human beings,
whose purpose and goal is the harnessing
and perfection of our sexual forces. A more
accurate translation of sexual magic would
be "sexual priesthood." In ancient times, the
priest was always accompanied by a priestess,
for they represent the divine forces at the base
of all creation: the masculine and feminine,
the Yab-Yum, Ying-Yang, Father-Mother:
the Elohim. Unfortunately, the term "sexual
magic" has been grossly misinterpreted by
mistaken persons such as Aleister Crowley, who
advocated a host of degenerated practices, all
of which belong solely to the lowest and most
perverse mentality and lead only to the enslave-
ment of the consciousness, the worship of lust
and desire, and the decay of humanity. True,
upright, heavenly sexual magic is the natural
harnessing of our latent forces, making them
active and harmonious with nature and the
divine, and which leads to the perfection of the
human being.

"People are filled with horror when they hear
about sexual magic; however, they are not filled
with horror when they give themselves to all
kinds of sexual perversion and to all kinds of
carnal passion." - Samael Aun Weor, *The Perfect
Matrimony*

Solar Bodies: The physical, vital, astral, mental, and causal bodies that are created through the beginning stages of Alchemy/Tantra and that provide a basis for existence in their corresponding levels of nature, just as the physical body does in the physical world. These bodies or vehicles are superior due to being created out of Solar (Christic) Energy, as opposed to the inferior, lunar bodies we receive from nature. Also known as the Wedding Garment (Christianity), the Merkabah (Kabbalah), To Soma Heliakon (Greek), and Sahu (Egyptian).

"All the Masters of the White Lodge, the Angels, Archangels, Thrones, Seraphim, Virtues, etc., etc., etc. are garbed with the Solar Bodies. Only those who have Solar Bodies have the Being incarnated. Only someone who possesses the Being is an authentic Human Being." - Samael Aun Weor, *The Esoteric Treatise of Hermetic Astrology*

White Fraternity, Lodge, or Brotherhood: That ancient collection of pure souls who maintain the highest and most sacred of sciences: White Magic or White Tantra. It is called White due to its purity and cleanliness. This "Brotherhood" or "Lodge" includes human beings of the highest order from every race, culture, creed and religion, and of both sexes.

Index